Cram101 Textbook Outlines to accompany:

# Western Civilization: Volume II: Since 1500

## Jackson J. Spielvogel, 7th Edition

A Cram101 Inc. publication (c) 2010.

# PRACTICE EXAMS.

Get all of the self-teaching practice exams for each chapter of this textbook at **www.Cram101.com** and ace the tests. Here is an example:

**Western Civilization: Volume II: Since 1500**
Jackson J. Spielvogel, 7th Edition,
**All Material Written and Prepared by Cram101**

I WANT A BETTER GRADE.

Items 1 - 50 of 100.

1 A _____ is an agricultural worker who subsists by working a small plot of ground. The term _____ today is sometimes used in a pejorative sense for impoverished farmers.

_____s typically make up the majority of the agricultural labour force in a Pre-industrial society, dependent on the cultivation of their land: without stockpiles of provisions they thrive or starve according to the most recent harvest.

- ○ Peasant
- ○ Pabst Plan
- ○ Pa Kao Her
- ○ Pachnamunis

2 The term _____ derives from the Latin imperium. Politically, an _____ is a geographically extensive group of states and peoples united and ruled either by a monarch (emperor, empress) or an oligarchy. Geopolitically, the term _____ has denoted very different, territorially-extreme states -- at the strong end, the extensive Spanish _____ and the British _____ (19th c)., at the weak end, the Holy Roman _____ (8th c.-19th c)., in its Medieval and early-modern forms, and the Byzantine _____ (15th c)., that was a direct continuation of the Roman _____, that, in its final century of existence, was more a city-state than a territorial _____.

- ○ Empire
- ○ Early Cholas
- ○ Earldom of Orkney
- ○ Early foundation

3 The _____ ) was a union of territories in Central Europe during the Middle Ages and the Early Modern period under a Holy Roman Emperor. The first emperor of the _____ was Otto I, crowned in 962. The last

You get a 50% discount for the online exams. Go to **Cram101.com**, click Sign Up at the top of the screen, and enter DK73DW6845 in the promo code box on the registration screen. Access to Cram101.com is $4.95 per month, cancel at any time.

With Cram101.com online, you also have access to extensive reference material.

You will nail those essays and papers. Here is an example from a Cram101 Biology text:

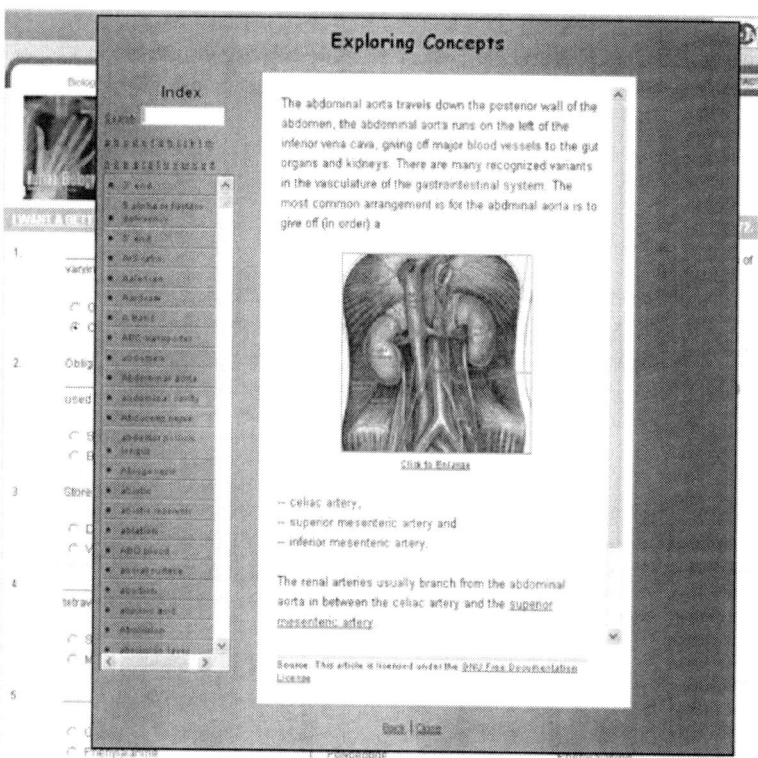

Visit **www.Cram101.com**, click Sign Up at the top of the screen, and enter DK73DW6845 in the promo code box on the registration screen. Access to www.Cram101.com is normally $9.95 per month, but because you have purchased this book, your access fee is only $4.95 per month, cancel at any time. Sign up and stop highlighting textbooks forever.

## Learning System

Cram101 Textbook Outlines is a learning system. The notes in this book are the highlights of your textbook, you will never have to highlight a book again.

**How to use this book.** Take this book to class, it is your notebook for the lecture. The notes and highlights on the left hand side of the pages follow the outline and order of the textbook. All you have to do is follow along while your instructor presents the lecture. Circle the items emphasized in class and add other important information on the right side. With Cram101 Textbook Outlines you'll spend less time writing and more time listening. Learning becomes more efficient.

## Cram101.com Online

Increase your studying efficiency by using Cram101.com's practice tests and online reference material. It is the perfect complement to Cram101 Textbook Outlines. Use self-teaching matching tests or simulate in-class testing with comprehensive multiple choice tests, or simply use Cram's true and false tests for quick review. Cram101.com even allows you to enter your in-class notes for an integrated studying format combining the textbook notes with your class notes.

Visit **www.Cram101.com**, click Sign Up at the top of the screen, and enter **DK73DW6845** in the promo code box on the registration screen. Access to www.Cram101.com is normally $9.95 per month, but because you have purchased this book, your access fee is only $4.95 per month. Sign up and stop highlighting textbooks forever.

Western Civilization: Volume II: Since 1500
Jackson J. Spielvogel, 7th

# CONTENTS

## Chapter 1. REFORMATION AND RELIGIOUS WARFARE IN THE SIXTEENTH CENTURY

| | |
|---|---|
| Peasant | A Peasant is an agricultural worker who subsists by working a small plot of ground. The term Peasant today is sometimes used in a pejorative sense for impoverished farmers. |
| | Peasants typically make up the majority of the agricultural labour force in a Pre-industrial society, dependent on the cultivation of their land: without stockpiles of provisions they thrive or starve according to the most recent harvest. |
| Empire | The term Empire derives from the Latin imperium. Politically, an Empire is a geographically extensive group of states and peoples united and ruled either by a monarch (emperor, empress) or an oligarchy. Geopolitically, the term Empire has denoted very different, territorially-extreme states -- at the strong end, the extensive Spanish Empire and the British Empire (19th c.)., at the weak end, the Holy Roman Empire (8th c.-19th c)., in its Medieval and early-modern forms, and the Byzantine Empire (15th c.)., that was a direct continuation of the Roman Empire, that, in its final century of existence, was more a city-state than a territorial Empire. |
| Holy Roman Empire | The Holy Roman Empire ) was a union of territories in Central Europe during the Middle Ages and the Early Modern period under a Holy Roman Emperor. The first emperor of the Holy Roman Empire was Otto I, crowned in 962. The last was Francis II, who abdicated and dissolved the Empire in 1806 during the Napoleonic Wars. |
| Roman | A Roman or civil diocese was one of the administrative divisions of the later Roman Empire, starting with the Tetrarchy. It formed the intermediate level of government, grouping several provinces and being in turn subordinated to a praetorian prefecture. |
| | The earliest use of "diocese" as an administrative unit was in the Greek-speaking East. |
| Koinon | The Koinon (or "League") of Free Laconians was established in 21 BC by the Emperor Augustus, giving formal structure to a group of cities that had been associated for almost two centuries. |
| | The Eleutherolakones (á¼˜λευθερολÎ¬κωνες, free Laconians) are first mentioned in 195 BC, after Sparta"s defeat in the Roman-Spartan War. The Roman general Titus Quinctius Flaminius placed several coastal cities of the Mani Peninsula under the protection of the Achean League, freeing them from Spartan hegemony. |
| Ottoman | The state of the Ottomans which began as part of the Anatolian Seljuk Sultanate and became an independent Empire, has been known historically by different names at different periods and in various languages. This page surveys the history of these names and their usage. |
| | · Modern Turkish: OsmanlÄ± BeyliÄŸi;<br>The first declaration of statehood happened under Osman I. |
| | · Ä€l-e Uá'mÄ n |

· Medieval Latin: Turchia
· Medieval Latin: Imperium Turcicum
· English: Turkey ; the current use of the name Turkey refers to the Republic of Turkey which succeeded the Ottoman Empire in 1923
· English: Turkish Empire, Ottoman Empire, Osmanic Empire, Osmanian Empire
· Ottoman Turkish/Persian: Ø¯Ù˘Ù„Ø Ø¹Ù„ÛŞÙ‡ Ø¹Ø«Ù…Ø§Ù†ÛŞÙ‡ Devlet-i Âliye-yi Osmâniyye
· Ottoman Turkish/Persian: Devlet-i Âliye (The Sublime State)
· Ottoman Turkish/Persian: Devlet-i Ebed-Müddet
· Ottoman Turkish/Persian: Memâlik-i Mahrûse (The Well-Protected Domains)
· Ottoman Turkish/Persian: Memâlik-i Mahrûse-i Osmanî
· Modern Turkish: OsmanlÄ± Ä°mparatorluÄŸu (Ottoman Empire),
· Arabic: Ø§Ù„Ø¯ÙˆÙ„Ø©Ù€ Ø§Ù„Ø¹Ù„ÙŞØ©Ù€ Ø§Ù„Ø¹Ø«Ù…Ø§Ù†ÙŞØ©Ù€ Ad-Dawlat al-Ë¤Ä€lÄ« al-Ë¤UthmÄ nÄ«
· Bulgarian: ÐžÑ Ð¼Ð°Ð½Ñ ÐºÐ° Ð¸Ð¼Ð¿ÐµÑ€Ð¸Ñ (Osmanska Imperia)
· Greek: ΟθωμανικΊ® ΑυτοκρατορΊ¯ α
· Armenian: Ö•Õ½Õ´Õ¡Õ¶Õ¶Õ¥Õ¡Õ¶ Õ¿Õ¡Õ¶Õ½Õ¯Õ¡Õ¯Õ¡Õ¶Õ¶ (Osmanyan Kaysroutyoun)

In diplomatic circles, the Ottoman government was often referred to as the "Sublime Porte", a literal translation of the Ottoman Turkish Bâb-Ä± Âlî, which was the only gate of the imperial TopkapÄ± Palace that was open to foreigners, and where the Sultan, Grand Vizier or Viziers greeted the ambassadors.

| | |
|---|---|
| Ottoman Empire | The Ottoman Empire or Ottoman State , also known by its contemporaries as the Turkish Empire or Turkey , was an empire that lasted from 1299 to November 1, 1922 (as an imperial monarchy) or July 24, 1923 (de jure, as a state.) It was succeeded by the Republic of Turkey, which was officially proclaimed on October 29, 1923. |
| | At the height of its power (16th-17th century), it spanned three continents, controlling much of Southeastern Europe, Western Asia and North Africa. |
| Swiss Confederation | Switzerland , officially the Swiss Confederation , is a federal republic consisting of 26 states named cantons, with Bern as the seat of the federal authorities. The country is situated in Western Europe where it is bordered by Germany to the north, France to the west, Italy to the south and Austria and Liechtenstein to the east. |
| | Switzerland is a landlocked country whose territory is geographically divided between the Jura, the Central Plateau and the Alps; adding together an area of 41,285 km$^2$. |
| Czechoslovakia | Czechoslovakia was a sovereign state in Central Europe which existed from October 1918, when it declared its independence from the Austro-Hungarian Empire, until 1992. From 1939 to 1945 the state did not have a de facto existence, due to its forced division and partial incorporation into Germany, but the Czech government-in-exile nevertheless continued to exist during this time period while Slovakia was independent from the Czech part. On 1 January 1993 Czechoslovakia peacefully split into the Czech Republic and Slovakia. |

| | |
|---|---|
| Liberal Party | Liberal Party is the name of dozens of political parties around the world. It usually designates a party that is ideologically liberal, meaning that they advocate individual rights and civil liberties, and sometimes left wing, meaning that they are reliant on governmental solutions to social and economic problems. There are also some Liberal Parties which subscribe to classical liberalism and therefore support a mostly unregulated free market. |
| Howard | Howard is a popular English language occupational given name of Old English origin, meaning "noble watchman". Its nickname is "Howie" and its shortened form is "Ward" . Between 1900-1960, Howard ranked in the U.S. Top 200; between 1960-1990, it ranked in the U.S. Top 400; between 1990-2004, it ranked in the U.S. Top 600. |
| Strasbourg | Strasbourg is the capital and principal city of the Alsace region in northeastern France. With 702,412 inhabitants in 2007, its metropolitan area is the ninth largest in France. Located close to the border with Germany, it is the capital of the Bas-Rhin department. |
| France | France or ; French: [fʁɑ̃Ê Éˈl ʃs]), officially the French Republic , is a country located in Western Europe, with several overseas islands and territories located on other continents. Metropolitan France extends from the Mediterranean Sea to the English Channel and the North Sea, and from the Rhine to the Atlantic Ocean. It is often referred to as L"Hexagone ("The Hexagon") because of the geometric shape of its territory. |
| Day | A Day (symbol d) is a unit of time equivalent to approximately 24 hours. It is not an SI unit but it is accepted for use with SI. The SI unit of time is the second. <br> The word "Day" can also refer to the (roughly) half of the Day that is not night, also known as "Daytime". |
| Cyprus | Cyprus , officially the Republic of Cyprus , is a Eurasian island country situated in the eastern Mediterranean, south of Turkey and west of Syria and Lebanon. <br> Cyprus is the Mediterranean"s third largest island, and one of its most popular tourist destinations, attracting over 2.4 million tourists per year. A former British colony, it became an independent republic in 1960 and a member of the Commonwealth in 1961. |
| Republic of the Seven United Netherlands | The Republic of the Seven United Netherlands (or "of the Seven United Provinces") was a European republic between 1581 and 1795, in about the same location as the modern Kingdom of the Netherlands, which is the successor state. <br> Before 1581, the area of the Low Countries consisted of a number of duchies, counties, and independent bishoprics, some but not all of them part of the Holy Roman Empire. Today that area is divided between the Netherlands, Belgium, Luxembourg and parts of France and Germany. |
| Union of Soviet Socialist Republics | The Union of Soviet Socialist Republics (USSR) was a constitutionally socialist state that existed in Eurasia from 1922 to 1991. The name is a translation of the Russian: Â·), tr. Soyuz Sovetskikh Sotsialisticheskikh Respublik, abbreviated Ð¡Ð¡Ð¡Ð , SSSR. The common short name is Soviet Union, from СÐ¾Ð¾²ÐµÑ‚Ñ ÐºÐ¸Ð¹ Ð¡Ð¾ÑŽÐ·, Sovetskiy Soyuz. |

Union of Utrecht

The Union of Utrecht (Dutch: Unie van Utrecht) was a treaty signed on 23 January 1579 in Utrecht, the Netherlands, unifying the northern provinces of the Netherlands, until then under the control of Spain. The Union of Utrecht is regarded as the foundation of the Republic of the Seven United Netherlands, which was not recognized by the Spanish Empire until the Twelve Years" Truce in 1609.

The treaty was signed on 23 January by Holland, Zeeland, Utrecht (but not all of Utrecht) and the province (but not the city) of Groningen.

| | |
|---|---|
| Portugal | Portugal , officially the Portuguese Republic (Portuguese: República Portuguesa), is a country on the Iberian Peninsula, member of the European Union and one of the founding members of NATO. Located in southwestern Europe, Portugal is the westernmost country of mainland Europe and is bordered by the Atlantic Ocean to the west and south and by Spain to the north and east. The Atlantic archipelagos of the Azores and Madeira are also part of Portugal. |
| | The land within the borders of today"s Portuguese Republic has been continuously settled since prehistoric times. |
| India | India, officially the Indian Empire, declared war on Germany in September 1939. The Provinces of India " href="/wiki/East_African_Campaign_(World_War_II)">East African Campaign, Western Desert Campaign and the Italian Campaign. At the height of the World War, more than 2.5 million Indian troops were fighting Axis forces around the globe. |
| Empire | The term Empire derives from the Latin imperium. Politically, an Empire is a geographically extensive group of states and peoples united and ruled either by a monarch (emperor, empress) or an oligarchy. Geopolitically, the term Empire has denoted very different, territorially-extreme states -- at the strong end, the extensive Spanish Empire and the British Empire (19th c.), at the weak end, the Holy Roman Empire (8th c.-19th c.), in its Medieval and early-modern forms, and the Byzantine Empire (15th c.), that was a direct continuation of the Roman Empire, that, in its final century of existence, was more a city-state than a territorial Empire. |
| Qing dynasty | The Qing Dynasty , also known as the Manchu Dynasty, was the last ruling dynasty of China, ruling from 1644 to 1912 " href="/wiki/Zhang_Xun_(Republic_of_China)">abortive restoration in 1917.) It was preceded by the Ming Dynasty and followed by the Republic. |
| | The dynasty was founded by the Manchu clan Aisin Gioro in what is today northeast China (also known as Manchuria.) |
| Spice trade | The Spice trade is a commercial activity of ancient origin which involves the merchandising of spices, incense, herbs, drugs and opium. Civilizations of Asia were involved in Spice trade from the ancient times, and the Greco-Roman world soon followed by trading along the Incense route and the Roman-India routes. The Roman-Indian routes were dependent upon techniques developed by the maritime trading power, Kingdom of Axum (ca 400s BC-AD 1000s) which had pioneered the Red Sea route before the 1st century. |
| Philippines | The Philippines (Tagalog: Pilipinas [pɛ^ɪɛ^ɐ^ɛ^pinɛ s]) officially known as the Republic of the Philippines, is a country in Southeast Asia with Manila as its capital city. It comprises 7,107 islands in the western Pacific Ocean. |
| | The Philippines is the world"s 12th most populous country, with an estimated population of about 92 million people. |
| Colonization | Colonization, , occurs whenever any one or more species populate an area. The term, which is derived from the Latin colere, "to inhabit, cultivate, frequent, practice, tend, guard, respect," originally related to humans. However, 19th century biogeographers dominated the term to describe the activities of birds, bacteria, or plant species. |

| | |
|---|---|
| Tenochtitlan | Tenochtitlan (Classical Nahuatl: TenÂ chtitlan [tenoË tÊʃÈˆtitÉ¬an]) (sometimes paired with Mexico as Mexico Tenochtitlan or Tenochtitlan Mexico) was a Nahua altepetl (city-state) located on an island in Lake Texcoco, in the Valley of Mexico. Founded in 1325, it became the seat of the growing Aztec empire in the 15th Century, until captured by the Spanish in 1521. It subsequently became a cabecera of the Viceroyalty of New Spain, and today the ruins of Tenochtitlan are located in the central part of Mexico City. |
| Peru | Peru , officially the Republic of Peru ), is a country in western South America. It is bordered on the north by Ecuador and Colombia, on the east by Brazil, on the southeast by Bolivia, on the south by Chile, and on the west by the Pacific Ocean.<br>Peruvian territory was home to the Norte Chico civilization, one of the oldest in the world, and to the Inca Empire, the largest state in Pre-Columbian America. The Spanish Empire conquered the region in the 16th century and established a Viceroyalty, which included most of its South American colonies. After achieving independence in 1821, Peru has undergone periods of political unrest and fiscal crisis as well as periods of stability and economic upswing. |
| Mountain | A Mountain is a large landform that stretches above the surrounding land in a limited area usually in the form of a peak. A Mountain is generally steeper than a hill. The adjective montane is used to describe Mountainous areas and things associated with them. |
| Viceroy | A Viceroy is a royal official who runs a country or province in the name of and as representative of the monarch. The term derives from the Latin prefix vice-, meaning "in the place of" and the French word roi, meaning king. His province or larger territory is called a Viceroyalty. |
| East India Company | The East India Company was an early English joint-stock company that was formed initially for pursuing trade with the East Indies, but that ended up trading mainly with the Indian subcontinent and China. The oldest among several similarly formed European East India Companies, the Company was granted an English Royal Charter, under the name Governor and Company of Merchants of London Trading into the East Indies, by Elizabeth I on 31 December 1600. After a rival English company challenged its monopoly in the late 17th century, the two companies were merged in 1708 to form the United Company of Merchants of England Trading to the East Indies, commonly styled the Honourable East India Company, and abbreviated, HEast India Company; the Company was colloquially referred to as John Company, and in India as Company Bahadur . |
| France | France or ; French: [fÊ É·Ìʃs]), officially the French Republic , is a country located in Western Europe, with several overseas islands and territories located on other continents. Metropolitan France extends from the Mediterranean Sea to the English Channel and the North Sea, and from the Rhine to the Atlantic Ocean. It is often referred to as L"Hexagone ("The Hexagon") because of the geometric shape of its territory. |

| | |
|---|---|
| Slavery | Slavery (Romanian: robie) existed on the territory of present-day Romania from before the founding of the principalities of Wallachia and Moldavia in 13th-14th century, until it was abolished in stages during the 1840s and 1850s. Most of the slaves were of Roma (Gypsy) ethnicity. Particularly in Moldavia there were also slaves of Tatar ethnicity, probably prisoners captured from the wars with the Nogai and Crimean Tatars. |
| Popular Front | A Popular Front is a broad coalition of different political groupings, often made up of leftists and centrists who are united by opposition to another group (most often capitalist groups). Being very broad, they can sometimes include centrist and liberal (or "bourgeois") forces as well as socialist and communist ("working-class") groups. Popular Fronts are larger in scope than united fronts, which contain only working-class groups. |
| Surat | Surat formerly known as Suryapur or Khubsoorat, is the Eighth largest city in India . The city proper is 7th most populous city in India and 49th in World. Surat is the administrative capital of Surat district and the 8th Metro city of India. |
| Colony | In politics and in history, a Colony is a territory under the immediate political control of a state. For colonies in antiquity, city-states would often found their own colonies. Some colonies were historically countries, while others were territories without definite statehood from their inception. |
| Ming dynasty | During the Ming dynasty in China attempts were made to subjugate, control, tax, and settle ethnic Chinese along the lightly populated frontier of Yunnan with Southeast Asia . This frontier region was inhabited by many small Tai chieftainships or states as well as other Tibeto-Burman and Mon-Khmer ethnic groups.<br><br>The Ming Shi-lu records the relations between the Ming court in Beijing and the Tai-Yunnan frontier as well as Ming military actions and diplomacy along the frontier. |
| Barbados | Barbados , situated just east of the Caribbean Sea, is an independent West Indian Continental Island-nation in the western Atlantic Ocean. For over three centuries Barbados was under British rule and maintains Queen Elizabeth II as head of state. Located at roughly 13° North of the equator and 59° West of the prime meridian, it is considered a part of the Lesser Antilles. |
| Guadeloupe | Guadeloupe (Antillean Creole: Gwadloup ; Tamil: à®•à¯ à®µà®¾à®¤à®²à¯ ,à®ªà¯ à®ªà¯ ‡) is an archipelago located in the eastern Caribbean Sea at 16°15′N 61°35′W / 16.25°N 61.583°W, with a land area of 1,628 square kilometres (629 sq. mi). It is an overseas department of France. |
| Japan | Japan participated in World War I from 1914 to 1917, as one of the major Entente Powers and played an important role in securing the sea lanes in South Pacific and Indian Oceans against the Kaiserliche Marine. Politically, Japan seized the opportunity to expand its sphere of influence in China, and to gain recognition as a great power in postwar geopolitics.<br><br>On 7 August 1914, the Japanese government received an official request from the British government for assistance in destroying the German raiders of the Kaiserliche Marine in and around Chinese waters. |

| | |
|---|---|
| Canada | CANADA is a country occupying most of northern North America, extending from the Atlantic Ocean in the east to the Pacific Ocean in the west and northward into the Arctic Ocean. It is the world"s second largest country by total area and shares the world"s longest common border with the United States to the south and northwest.<br>The land occupied by CANADA was inhabited for millennia by various groups of Aboriginal people. |
| French colonies | "French Colonies" is the name used by philatelists to refer to the postage stamps issued by France for use in the parts of the French colonial empire that did not have stamps of their own. These were in use from 1859 to 1906, and from 1943 to 1945. French Colonies stamp 1859<br>The first of these were small square stamps issued in 1859, depicting an eagle and crown in a round frame, with the inscription "COLONIES DE L"EMPIRE FRANCAIS". |
| Lawrence | Lawrence is a city in Essex County, Massachusetts, United States on the Merrimack River. As of the 2000 census, the city had a total population of 72,043. Surrounding communities include Methuen to the north, Andover to the southwest, and North Andover to the southeast. |
| Massachusetts | The Commonwealth of Massachusetts () is a state in the New England region of the northeastern United States. It is bordered by Rhode Island and Connecticut to the south, New York to the west, and Vermont and New Hampshire to the north; at its east lies the Atlantic Ocean. Most of its population of 6.4 million lives in the Boston metropolitan area. |
| New Netherland | · Fort Amsterdam<br>· Fort Nassau (North)<br>· Fort Orange<br><br>· Fort Nassau (South)<br>· Fort Goede Hoop<br>· De Wal<br><br>· Fort Casimir<br>· Fort Altena<br>· Fort Wilhelmus<br>· Fort Beversreede<br>· Fort Nya Korsholm<br>· De Rondout |

Settlements:

- Noten Eylandt
- New Amsterdam
- Rensselaerswyck
- New Haarlem
- Noortwyck
- Beverwyck
- Wiltwyck
- Bergen
- Pavonia
- Vriessendael
- Achter Col
- Vlissingen
- Oude Dorpe

- Colen Donck
- Greenwich
- Heemstede
- Rustdorp
- Gravesende
- Breuckelen
- New Amersfoort
- Midwout
- New Utrecht
- Boswyck
- Swaanendael
- New Amstel
- Nieuw Dorp

## The Patroon System

Charter of Freedoms and Exemptions

## Directors of New Netherland:

Cornelius Jacobsen Mey (1620-25)

Willem Verhulst (1625-26)

Peter Minuit (1626-32)

Sebastiaen Jansen Krol(1632-33)

Wouter van Twiller (1633-38)

Willem Kieft (1638-47)

Peter Stuyvesant (1647-64)

## People of New Netherland

New Netherland, or Nieuw-Nederland in Dutch, was the seventeenth-century colonial province of the Republic of the Seven United Netherlands on the East Coast of North America. The claimed territories were the lands from the Delmarva Peninsula to extreme southwestern Cape Cod. The settled areas are now part of the Mid-Atlantic States of New York, New Jersey, Delaware, and Connecticut, with small outposts in Pennsylvania and Rhode Island. Its capital, New Amsterdam, was located at the southern tip of the island of Manhattan on Upper New York Bay.

New Netherlander

Twelve Men

Eight Men

Nine Men

Flushing Remonstrance

| | |
|---|---|
| New York | New York is a state in the Mid-Atlantic and Northeastern regions of the United States and is the nation"s third most populous. The state is bordered by New Jersey and Pennsylvania to the south, and Connecticut, Massachusetts and Vermont to the east. The state has a maritime border with Rhode Island east of Long Island, as well as an international border with the Canadian provinces of Ontario to the west, and Quebec to the north. |
| Revolution | A Revolution is a fundamental change in power or organizational structures that takes place in a relatively short period of time. Aristotle described two types of political Revolution<br><br>· Complete change from one constitution to another<br>· Modification of an existing constitution.<br>Revolution s have occurred through human history and vary widely in terms of methods, duration, and motivating ideology. |
| Fugger | The Fugger family was a historically prominent group of European bankers, members of the fifteenth and sixteenth-century mercantile patriciate of Augsburg, international mercantile bankers, and venture capitalists like the Welser and the Höchstetter families.<br>The first reference to the Fugger family in the Swabian Free City of Augsburg is the arrival of Hans Fugger recorded in the tax register of 1357. He married Klara Widolf and became an Augsburg citizen. |
| Peasant | A Peasant is an agricultural worker who subsists by working a small plot of ground. The term Peasant today is sometimes used in a pejorative sense for impoverished farmers.<br>Peasants typically make up the majority of the agricultural labour force in a Pre-industrial society, dependent on the cultivation of their land: without stockpiles of provisions they thrive or starve according to the most recent harvest. |

France

France or ; French: [fɛ̃ ɛˈ]fs]), officially the French Republic , is a country located in Western Europe, with several overseas islands and territories located on other continents. Metropolitan France extends from the Mediterranean Sea to the English Channel and the North Sea, and from the Rhine to the Atlantic Ocean. It is often referred to as L"Hexagone ("The Hexagon") because of the geometric shape of its territory.

Koinon

The Koinon (or "League") of Free Laconians was established in 21 BC by the Emperor Augustus, giving formal structure to a group of cities that had been associated for almost two centuries.
The Eleutherolakones (ἀ¼ˉλευθερολÎ¬κωνες, free Laconians) are first mentioned in 195 BC, after Sparta"s defeat in the Roman-Spartan War. The Roman general Titus Quinctius Flaminius placed several coastal cities of the Mani Peninsula under the protection of the Achean League, freeing them from Spartan hegemony.

Toul

Toul is a commune in the Meurthe-et-Moselle department in northeastern France.
It is a sub-prefecture of the department.

Revolution

A Revolution is a fundamental change in power or organizational structures that takes place in a relatively short period of time. Aristotle described two types of political Revolution

· Complete change from one constitution to another
· Modification of an existing constitution.
Revolution s have occurred through human history and vary widely in terms of methods, duration, and motivating ideology.

Peasant

A Peasant is an agricultural worker who subsists by working a small plot of ground. The term Peasant today is sometimes used in a pejorative sense for impoverished farmers.
Peasants typically make up the majority of the agricultural labour force in a Pre-industrial society, dependent on the cultivation of their land: without stockpiles of provisions they thrive or starve according to the most recent harvest.

Portugal

Portugal , officially the Portuguese Republic (Portuguese: República Portuguesa), is a country on the Iberian Peninsula, member of the European Union and one of the founding members of NATO. Located in southwestern Europe, Portugal is the westernmost country of mainland Europe and is bordered by the Atlantic Ocean to the west and south and by Spain to the north and east. The Atlantic archipelagos of the Azores and Madeira are also part of Portugal.
The land within the borders of today"s Portuguese Republic has been continuously settled since prehistoric times.

Rebellion

Rebellion is a refusal of obedience. It may, therefore, be seen as encompassing a range of behaviors from civil disobedience and mass nonviolent resistance, to violent and organized attempts to destroy an established authority such as the government. Those who participate in Rebellions are known as "rebels".

| | |
|---|---|
| Politics | Politics is a process by which groups of people make decisions. The term is generally applied to behavior within civil governments, but Politics has been observed in all human group interactions, including corporate, academic and religious institutions. It consists of "social relations involving authority or power" and refers to the regulation of a political unit, and to the methods and tactics used to formulate and apply policy. |
| Slavery | Slavery (Romanian: robie) existed on the territory of present-day Romania from before the founding of the principalities of Wallachia and Moldavia in 13th-14th century, until it was abolished in stages during the 1840s and 1850s. Most of the slaves were of Roma (Gypsy) ethnicity. Particularly in Moldavia there were also slaves of Tatar ethnicity, probably prisoners captured from the wars with the Nogai and Crimean Tatars. |
| Austria | Austria ), officially the Republic of Austria , is a landlocked country of roughly 8.3 million people in Central Europe. It borders both Germany and the Czech Republic to the north, Slovakia and Hungary to the east, Slovenia and Italy to the south, and Switzerland and Liechtenstein to the west. The territory of Austria covers 83,872 square kilometres (32,383 sq mi), and is influenced by a temperate and alpine climate. |
| Empire | The term Empire derives from the Latin imperium. Politically, an Empire is a geographically extensive group of states and peoples united and ruled either by a monarch (emperor, empress) or an oligarchy. Geopolitically, the term Empire has denoted very different, territorially-extreme states -- at the strong end, the extensive Spanish Empire and the British Empire (19th c.), at the weak end, the Holy Roman Empire (8th c.-19th c.), in its Medieval and early-modern forms, and the Byzantine Empire (15th c.), that was a direct continuation of the Roman Empire, that, in its final century of existence, was more a city-state than a territorial Empire. |
| Holy Roman Empire | The Holy Roman Empire ) was a union of territories in Central Europe during the Middle Ages and the Early Modern period under a Holy Roman Emperor. The first emperor of the Holy Roman Empire was Otto I, crowned in 962. The last was Francis II, who abdicated and dissolved the Empire in 1806 during the Napoleonic Wars. |
| Roman | A Roman or civil diocese was one of the administrative divisions of the later Roman Empire, starting with the Tetrarchy. It formed the intermediate level of government, grouping several provinces and being in turn subordinated to a praetorian prefecture. The earliest use of "diocese" as an administrative unit was in the Greek-speaking East. |
| Strasbourg | Strasbourg is the capital and principal city of the Alsace region in northeastern France. With 702,412 inhabitants in 2007, its metropolitan area is the ninth largest in France. Located close to the border with Germany, it is the capital of the Bas-Rhin department. |

| | |
|---|---|
| Congress | The 2001 Congress of the Greens/Green Party USA, held at Carbondale, Illinois, was a critical event in the history of the Green Party in the United States. At the Congress, occurring July 20 to July 23, at which the G/GPUSA was to consider the Boston Proposal , a tentative "merger" agreement between it and the Association of State Green Parties (ASGP). After an intense internal organizational struggle, most of which revolved around whether or not to "accredit" various delegations (and thus grant the individuals within them voting privileges), the proposal was rejected; although 55% of the members in attendance voted to approve it (99 in favor, 81 against), the organization"s bylaws required yes votes from a "super-majority" of 66.7% of the delegates in attendance to pass. |
| Nova Scotia | Nova Scotia is a Canadian province located on Canada"s southeastern coast. It is the most populous province in Atlantic Canada. Its capital, Halifax, is a major economic centre of the region. |
| Brandenburg-Prussia | Brandenburg-Prussia was a German monarchy established by the personal union between the Duchy of Prussia and the Margraviate of Brandenburg in 1618.<br><br>The monarchy was ruled by the branch of the Hohenzollern dynasty that had earlier ruled Brandenburg. The term Brandenburg-Prussia refers to this monarchy from its establishment until 1701, after which it is usually known as the Kingdom of Prussia. |
| Estates-General | The Estates-General (or States-General) of 1789 was the first meeting since 1614 of the French Estates-General, a general assembly representing the French collection of peoples. The independence from the Crown which it displayed paved the way for the French Revolution.<br><br>Among the direct causes of the French Revolution was a massive financial crisis caused by France"s enormous national debt, the lack of food and its outrageous prices, the desire to imitate the American Revolution, the government"s lavish spending, and an archaic system of taxation which brought little money to the national coffers though placing the tax burden upon the Third Estate , while virtually ignoring the First Estate (the Clergy) and the Second Estate (the Nobility). |
| Austrian Empire | The Austrian Empire was a modern era successor empire founded on a remnant of the Holy Roman Empire centered on what is today"s Austria that officially lasted from 1804 to 1867. It was followed by combining the Royal House with that of Hungary creating the dual monarchy Austria-Hungary , which itself as one of the losers was dissolved at the end of World War I and broken into separate new states). The term "Austrian Empire" is also used for the Habsburg possessions before 1804, which had no official collective name, although Austria is more frequent; the term of Austria-Hungary has also been used, incorrectly. |
| Mantua | Mantua (Italian: Màntova, in the local dialect of Emilian language Mantua) is a city in Lombardy, Italy and capital of the province of the same name.<br><br>Mantua is surrounded on three sides by artificial lakes created during the 12th century. These receive the waters from the Mincio, which descend from Lake Garda. |
| Ottoman | The state of the Ottomans which began as part of the Anatolian Seljuk Sultanate and became an independent Empire, has been known historically by different names at different periods and in various languages. This page surveys the history of these names and their usage. |

· Modern Turkish: OsmanlÄ± BeyliÄŸi;
The first declaration of statehood happened under Osman I.

· Ä€l-e Uá¹mÄ n

· Medieval Latin: Turchia
· Medieval Latin: Imperium Turcicum
· English: Turkey ; the current use of the name Turkey refers to the Republic of Turkey which succeeded the Ottoman Empire in 1923
· English: Turkish Empire, Ottoman Empire, Osmanic Empire, Osmanian Empire
· Ottoman Turkish/Persian: Ø¯ÙˆÙ„Øª Ø¹Ù„ÙŠÙ‡ Ø¹Ø«Ù…Ø§Ù†ÙŠÙ‡ Devlet-i Âliye-yi Osmâniyye
· Ottoman Turkish/Persian: Devlet-i Âliye (The Sublime State)
· Ottoman Turkish/Persian: Devlet-i Ebed-Müddet
· Ottoman Turkish/Persian: Memâlik-i Mahrûse (The Well-Protected Domains)
· Ottoman Turkish/Persian: Memâlik-i Mahrûse-i Osmanî
· Modern Turkish: OsmanlÄ± Ä°mparatorluÄŸu (Ottoman Empire),
· Arabic: Ø§Ù„Ø¯ÙˆÙ„Ø©Ù€ Ø§Ù„Ø¹Ù„ÙŠØ©Ù€ Ø§Ù„Ø¹Ø«Ù…Ø§Ù†ÙŠØ©Ù€ Ad-Dawlat al-Ë¤Ä€lÄ« al-Ë¤UthmÄ nÄ«
· Bulgarian: ÐžÑ Ð¼Ð°Ð½Ñ ÐºÐ° Ð¸Ð¼Ð¿ÐµÑ€Ð¸Ñ (Osmanska Imperia)
· Greek: ÎŸθωμανικÎ® Î'Ï…Ï"οκρατορÎ" α
· Armenian: Ô•·Õ½Õ´Õ¡Õ¶ÕµÕ¡Õ¶ Õ¿Õ¡Õ¥Õ½Õ¶Õ¸Ö‚Õ©Õ©Õ¸Ö‚Õ¶ (Osmanyan Kaysroutyoun)
In diplomatic circles, the Ottoman government was often referred to as the "Sublime Porte", a literal translation of the Ottoman Turkish Bâb-Ä± Âlî, which was the only gate of the imperial TopkapÄ± Palace that was open to foreigners, and where the Sultan, Grand Vizier or Viziers greeted the ambassadors.

**Ottoman Empire**

The Ottoman Empire or Ottoman State , also known by its contemporaries as the Turkish Empire or Turkey , was an empire that lasted from 1299 to November 1, 1922 (as an imperial monarchy) or July 24, 1923 (de jure, as a state.) It was succeeded by the Republic of Turkey, which was officially proclaimed on October 29, 1923.
At the height of its power (16th-17th century), it spanned three continents, controlling much of Southeastern Europe, Western Asia and North Africa.

**Michael**

Michael is a given name that comes from the Hebrew: žÖ´×™×›Ö¸× Öµ×œ / ×ž×™×›×™× ×œâ€Ž , meaning "Who is like God?" In English, it is sometimes shortened to Mike, Mikey, or, especially in Ireland, Mick.
Michael is one of the Archangels.
Female forms of Michael include Michele, Michelle, Michaela, Mechelle, Micheline, and Michaelle, although there are women with the name Michael, such as Michael Learned.

| | |
|---|---|
| October | October Â·) is the tenth month of the year in the Gregorian Calendar and one of seven Gregorian months with a length of 31 days. The eighth month in the old Roman calendar, October retained its name when January and February were added. When the calendar was originally created by the Romans, the year began in March this meant that instead of October being the 10th month of the year it was originally the 8th month of the year. |
| Tsar | Tsar or czar , Ukrainian: Ñ†Đ°Ñ€, in Serbian: Ñ†Đ°Ñ€ / car, in scientific transliteration respectively car" and car), occasionally spelled csar or tzar in English, is a Slavic term with Bulgarian origins used to designate certain monarchs. The first ruler to adopt the title Tsar was Simeon I of Bulgaria Originally, the title Czar " href="/wiki/Caesar_(title)">Caesar) meant Emperor in the European medieval sense of the term, that is, a ruler who claims the same rank as a Roman emperor, with the approval of another emperor or a supreme ecclesiastical official (the Pope or the Ecumenical Patriarch). Occasionally, the word could be used to designate other, non-Christian, supreme rulers. |
| Union of Soviet Socialist Republics | The Union of Soviet Socialist Republics (USSR) was a constitutionally socialist state that existed in Eurasia from 1922 to 1991. The name is a translation of the Russian: Â·), tr. Soyuz Sovetskikh Sotsialisticheskikh Respublik, abbreviated Đ¡Đ¡Đ¡Đ , SSSR. The common short name is Soviet Union, from Đ¡Đ¾Đ²ĐµÑ‚Ñ ĐºĐ¸Đ¹ Đ¡Đ¾ÑŽĐ·, Sovetskiy Soyuz. |
| Austria-Hungary | Austria-Hungary the Dual Monarchy or the k.u.k Monarchy, was a state in Central Europe ruled by the House of Habsburg, constitutionally a monarchic union between the crowns of the Austrian Empire and the Kingdom of Hungary. The state was a result of the Ausgleich or Compromise of 1867, under which the Austrian Habsburgs agreed to share power with a separate Hungarian government, dividing the territory of the former Austrian Empire between them. The Dual Monarchy existed for 51 years until 1918, when it dissolved following military defeat in the First World War. |
| Republic of the Seven United Netherlands | The Republic of the Seven United Netherlands (or "of the Seven United Provinces") was a European republic between 1581 and 1795, in about the same location as the modern Kingdom of the Netherlands, which is the successor state. Before 1581, the area of the Low Countries consisted of a number of duchies, counties, and independent bishoprics, some but not all of them part of the Holy Roman Empire. Today that area is divided between the Netherlands, Belgium, Luxembourg and parts of France and Germany. |
| Liberal Party | Liberal Party is the name of dozens of political parties around the world. It usually designates a party that is ideologically liberal, meaning that they advocate individual rights and civil liberties, and sometimes left wing, meaning that they are reliant on governmental solutions to social and economic problems. There are also some Liberal Parties which subscribe to classical liberalism and therefore support a mostly unregulated free market. |
| Oireachtas | From 1922 to 1937 the Oireachtas was the legislature of the Irish Free State. Until the final days of the Irish Free State it consisted of the King and two houses: Dáil Éireann and Seanad Éireann (also known as the "Senate"). |

Like the modern Oireachtas, the Free State legislature was dominated by the powerful, directly elected Dáil.

| | |
|---|---|
| Levellers | The Levellers were a political movement during the English Civil Wars which emphasised popular sovereignty, extended suffrage, equality before the law, and religious tolerance, all of which were expressed in the manifesto "Agreement of the People". They were one of the largest factions on the Parliamentarian side during the English Civil Wars. They came to prominence at the end of the First English Civil War and were most influential before the start of the Second Civil War. |
| Glorious Revolution | The Glorious Revolution was the overthrow of King James II of England in 1688 by a union of Parliamentarians with an invading army led by the Dutch stadtholder William III of Orange-Nassau who as a result ascended the English throne as William III of England. The expression "Glorious Revolution" was first used by John Hampden in late 1689, and is an expression that is still used by the Westminster Parliament.<br><br>The Glorious Revolution is also occasionally termed the Bloodless Revolution, albeit inaccurately. |
| Mari | Mari (modern Tell Hariri, Syria) was an ancient Sumerian and Amorite city, located 11 kilometers north-west of the modern town of Abu Kamal on the western bank of Euphrates river, some 120 km southeast of Deir ez-Zor, Syria. It is thought to have been inhabited since the 5th millennium BC, although it flourished from 2900 BC until 1759 BC, when it was sacked by Hammurabi.<br><br>Mari was discovered in 1933 on the eastern flank of Syria, near the Iraqi border. |
| Popular Front | A Popular Front is a broad coalition of different political groupings, often made up of leftists and centrists who are united by opposition to another group (most often capitalist groups). Being very broad, they can sometimes include centrist and liberal (or "bourgeois") forces as well as socialist and communist ("working-class") groups. Popular Fronts are larger in scope than united fronts, which contain only working-class groups. |

| | |
|---|---|
| Revolution | A Revolution is a fundamental change in power or organizational structures that takes place in a relatively short period of time. Aristotle described two types of political Revolution<br><br>· Complete change from one constitution to another<br>· Modification of an existing constitution.<br>Revolution s have occurred through human history and vary widely in terms of methods, duration, and motivating ideology. |
| Scientific Revolution | In the history of science, the Scientific revolution was a period when new ideas in physics, astronomy, biology, human anatomy, chemistry, and other sciences led to a rejection of doctrines that had prevailed from Ancient Greece through the Middle Ages, and laid the foundation of modern science. According to the majority of scholars, the Scientific revolution began with the publication of two works that changed the course of science in 1543 and continued through the late 17th century: Nicolaus Copernicus"s De revolutionibus orbium coelestium (On the Revolutions of the Heavenly Spheres) and Andreas Vesalius"s De humani corporis fabrica (On the Fabric of the Human body.)<br>Philosopher and historian Alexandre Koyré coined the term Scientific revolution in 1939 to describe this epoch. |
| Aristocracy | Aristocracy is a form of government, in which a select few such as the most wise, strong or contributing citizens rule, often starting as a system of co-option where a council of prominent citizens add leading soldiers, merchants, land owners, priests, or lawyers to their number. Aristocracy deforms when it becomes hereditary elite.<br>Aristocracies have most often been deformed to hereditary plutocratic systems. |
| Scientific method | Scientific method refers to a body of techniques for investigating phenomena, acquiring new knowledge, or correcting and integrating previous knowledge. To be termed scientific, a method of inquiry must be based on gathering observable, empirical and measurable evidence subject to specific principles of reasoning. A Scientific method consists of the collection of data through observation and experimentation, and the formulation and testing of hypotheses. |

| | |
|---|---|
| Australia | Australia , officially the Commonwealth of Australia, is a country in the Southern Hemisphere comprising the continental mainland (the world"s smallest), the island of Tasmania, and numerous smaller islands in the Indian and Pacific Oceans.[N4] Neighbouring countries include Indonesia, East Timor, and Papua New Guinea to the north, the Solomon Islands, Vanuatu, and New Caledonia to the north-east, and New Zealand to the southeast. |
| | For some 40,000 years before European settlement commenced in the late 18th century, the Australian mainland and Tasmania were inhabited by around 250 individual nations of indigenous Australians. After sporadic visits by fishermen from the immediate north, and European discovery by Dutch explorers in 1606, the eastern half of Australia was claimed by the British in 1770 and initially settled through penal transportation to the colony of New South Wales, founded on 26 January 1788. |
| Law | The great end, for which men entered into society, was to secure their property. That right is preserved sacred and incommunicable in all instances, where it has not been taken away or abridged by some public Law for the good of the whole ... If no excuse can be found or produced, the silence of the books is an authority against the defendant, and the plaintiff must have judgment. |
| Nation | A nation is a body of people who share a real or imagined common history, culture, language or ethnic origin, who typically inhabit a particular country or territory. The development and conceptualization of the nation is closely related to the development of modern industrial states and nationalist movements in Europe in the 18th and 19th centuries, although nationalists would trace nations into the past along an uninterrupted lines of historical narrative. |
| | Benedict Anderson argued that nations were "imagined communities" because "the members of even the smallest nation will never know most of their fellow-members, meet them, or even hear of them, yet in the minds of each lives the image of their communion", and traced their origins back to vernacular print journalism, which by its very nature was limited with linguistic zones and addressed a common audience. |
| Force | In physics, a Force is any external agent that causes a change in the motion of a free body, or that causes stress in a fixed body. It can also be described by intuitive concepts such as a push or pull that can cause an object with mass to change its velocity , i.e., to accelerate, or which can cause a flexible object to deform. Force has both magnitude and direction, making it a vector quantity. |
| Liberalism | This article gives information on liberalism in diverse countries around the world. It is an overview of parties that adhere more or less (explicitly) to the ideas of political liberalism and is therefore a list of liberal parties around the world. |
| | One can argue what a liberal party is. |
| African Americans | Due to the prevailing social climate that existed in the United States after World War II, one in which racism was a prominent factor, African Americans did not benefit from the provisions of the G. I. Bill of Rights as much as their white counterparts. Though the bill did provide a more level playing field than the one blacks faced during Reconstruction, this is not saying much. Representative John Elliott Rankin, an economic liberal who was also an avid segregationalist and racist, sponsored the bill in the United States House of Representatives. |

| | |
|---|---|
| Republic of the Seven United Netherlands | The Republic of the Seven United Netherlands (or "of the Seven United Provinces") was a European republic between 1581 and 1795, in about the same location as the modern Kingdom of the Netherlands, which is the successor state.<br>Before 1581, the area of the Low Countries consisted of a number of duchies, counties, and independent bishoprics, some but not all of them part of the Holy Roman Empire. Today that area is divided between the Netherlands, Belgium, Luxembourg and parts of France and Germany. |
| History | · History of the East Coast of the United States<br>· History of the Southern United States<br>· History of the United States<br>· List of National Historic Landmarks in North Carolina<br>· National Register of Historic Places listings in North Carolina |
| Regions | |
| Larger cities | |
| Smaller cities | |
| Major Towns | |
| Counties | |
| Liberal Party | Liberal Party is the name of dozens of political parties around the world. It usually designates a party that is ideologically liberal, meaning that they advocate individual rights and civil liberties, and sometimes left wing, meaning that they are reliant on governmental solutions to social and economic problems. There are also some Liberal Parties which subscribe to classical liberalism and therefore support a mostly unregulated free market. |
| Empire | The term Empire derives from the Latin imperium. Politically, an Empire is a geographically extensive group of states and peoples united and ruled either by a monarch (emperor, empress) or an oligarchy. Geopolitically, the term Empire has denoted very different, territorially-extreme states -- at the strong end, the extensive Spanish Empire and the British Empire (19th c।)., at the weak end, the Holy Roman Empire (8th c.-19th c)., in its Medieval and early-modern forms, and the Byzantine Empire (15th c)., that was a direct continuation of the Roman Empire, that, in its final century of existence, was more a city-state than a territorial Empire. |
| Roman | A Roman or civil diocese was one of the administrative divisions of the later Roman Empire, starting with the Tetrarchy. It formed the intermediate level of government, grouping several provinces and being in turn subordinated to a praetorian prefecture.<br>The earliest use of "diocese" as an administrative unit was in the Greek-speaking East. |

Roman Empire

The Roman Empire was the post-Republican phase of the ancient Roman civilization, characterised by an autocratic form of government and large territorial holdings in Europe and around the Mediterranean. The term is used to describe the Roman state during and after the time of the first emperor, Augustus. The nearly 500-year-old Roman Republic, which preceded it, had been weakened by several civil wars.

Popular Front

A Popular Front is a broad coalition of different political groupings, often made up of leftists and centrists who are united by opposition to another group (most often capitalist groups). Being very broad, they can sometimes include centrist and liberal (or "bourgeois") forces as well as socialist and communist ("working-class") groups. Popular Fronts are larger in scope than united fronts, which contain only working-class groups.

| | |
|---|---|
| Declaration of Independence | A Declaration of independence is an assertion of the independence of an aspiring state or states. Such places are usually declared from part or all of the territory of another nation or failed nation, or are breakaway territories from within the larger state. Not all declarations of independence were successful and resulted in independence for these regions. |
| Law | The great end, for which men entered into society, was to secure their property. That right is preserved sacred and incommunicable in all instances, where it has not been taken away or abridged by some public Law for the good of the whole ... If no excuse can be found or produced, the silence of the books is an authority against the defendant, and the plaintiff must have judgment. |
| France | France or ; French: [fɛ́ É'lʃs]), officially the French Republic , is a country located in Western Europe, with several overseas islands and territories located on other continents. Metropolitan France extends from the Mediterranean Sea to the English Channel and the North Sea, and from the Rhine to the Atlantic Ocean. It is often referred to as L"Hexagone ("The Hexagon") because of the geometric shape of its territory. |
| Liberal Party | Liberal Party is the name of dozens of political parties around the world. It usually designates a party that is ideologically liberal, meaning that they advocate individual rights and civil liberties, and sometimes left wing, meaning that they are reliant on governmental solutions to social and economic problems. There are also some Liberal Parties which subscribe to classical liberalism and therefore support a mostly unregulated free market. |
| Mari | Mari (modern Tell Hariri, Syria) was an ancient Sumerian and Amorite city, located 11 kilometers north-west of the modern town of Abu Kamal on the western bank of Euphrates river, some 120 km southeast of Deir ez-Zor, Syria. It is thought to have been inhabited since the 5th millennium BC, although it flourished from 2900 BC until 1759 BC, when it was sacked by Hammurabi.<br>Mari was discovered in 1933 on the eastern flank of Syria, near the Iraqi border. |
| Oireachtas | From 1922 to 1937 the Oireachtas was the legislature of the Irish Free State. Until the final days of the Irish Free State it consisted of the King and two houses: Dáil Éireann and Seanad Éireann (also known as the "Senate").<br>Like the modern Oireachtas, the Free State legislature was dominated by the powerful, directly elected Dáil. |
| United Kingdom | The United Kingdom is a charter member of the United Nations and one of five permanent members of the UN Security Council.<br>The term "United Nations" was suggested by Franklin D. Roosevelt to Winston Churchill during World War II, to refer to the Allies. It appeared in the Declaration by the United Nations where, on 1 January 1942, 26 nations pledged to continue fighting the Axis powers. |

| | |
|---|---|
| Austria-Hungary | Austria-Hungary the Dual Monarchy or the k.u.k Monarchy, was a state in Central Europe ruled by the House of Habsburg, constitutionally a monarchic union between the crowns of the Austrian Empire and the Kingdom of Hungary. The state was a result of the Ausgleich or Compromise of 1867, under which the Austrian Habsburgs agreed to share power with a separate Hungarian government, dividing the territory of the former Austrian Empire between them. The Dual Monarchy existed for 51 years until 1918, when it dissolved following military defeat in the First World War. |
| Republic of the Seven United Netherlands | The Republic of the Seven United Netherlands (or "of the Seven United Provinces") was a European republic between 1581 and 1795, in about the same location as the modern Kingdom of the Netherlands, which is the successor state. <br><br> Before 1581, the area of the Low Countries consisted of a number of duchies, counties, and independent bishoprics, some but not all of them part of the Holy Roman Empire. Today that area is divided between the Netherlands, Belgium, Luxembourg and parts of France and Germany. |
| Peasant | A Peasant is an agricultural worker who subsists by working a small plot of ground. The term Peasant today is sometimes used in a pejorative sense for impoverished farmers. <br><br> Peasants typically make up the majority of the agricultural labour force in a Pre-industrial society, dependent on the cultivation of their land: without stockpiles of provisions they thrive or starve according to the most recent harvest. |
| Austria | Austria ), officially the Republic of Austria , is a landlocked country of roughly 8.3 million people in Central Europe. It borders both Germany and the Czech Republic to the north, Slovakia and Hungary to the east, Slovenia and Italy to the south, and Switzerland and Liechtenstein to the west. The territory of Austria covers 83,872 square kilometres (32,383 sq mi), and is influenced by a temperate and alpine climate. |
| Charter | A Charter is the grant of authority or rights, stating that the granter formally recognizes the prerogative of the recipient to exercise the rights specified. It is implicit that the granter retains superiority (or sovereignty), and that the recipient admits a limited (or inferior) status within the relationship, and it is within that sense that Charters were historically granted, and that sense is retained in modern usage of the term. Also, Charter can simply be a document giving royal permission to start a colony. |
| Rebellion | Rebellion is a refusal of obedience. It may, therefore, be seen as encompassing a range of behaviors from civil disobedience and mass nonviolent resistance, to violent and organized attempts to destroy an established authority such as the government. Those who participate in Rebellions are known as "rebels". |

Congress

The 2001 Congress of the Greens/Green Party USA, held at Carbondale, Illinois, was a critical event in the history of the Green Party in the United States. At the Congress, occurring July 20 to July 23, at which the G/GPUSA was to consider the Boston Proposal , a tentative "merger" agreement between it and the Association of State Green Parties (ASGP). After an intense internal organizational struggle, most of which revolved around whether or not to "accredit" various delegations (and thus grant the individuals within them voting privileges), the proposal was rejected; although 55% of the members in attendance voted to approve it (99 in favor, 81 against), the organization"s bylaws required yes votes from a "super-majority" of 66.7% of the delegates in attendance to pass.

Ottoman

The state of the Ottomans which began as part of the Anatolian Seljuk Sultanate and became an independent Empire, has been known historically by different names at different periods and in various languages. This page surveys the history of these names and their usage.

· Modern Turkish: OsmanlÄ± BeyliÄŸi;

The first declaration of statehood happened under Osman I.

· Ä€l-e Uá¹mÄ  n

· Medieval Latin: Turchia
· Medieval Latin: Imperium Turcicum
· English: Turkey ; the current use of the name Turkey refers to the Republic of Turkey which succeeded the Ottoman Empire in 1923
· English: Turkish Empire, Ottoman Empire, Osmanic Empire, Osmanian Empire
· Ottoman Turkish/Persian: Ø¯ÙˆÙ„Øª Ø¹Ù„ÙŠÙ‡ Ø¹Ø«Ù…Ø§Ù†ÙŠÙ‡ Devlet-i Âliye-yi Osmâniyye
· Ottoman Turkish/Persian: Devlet-i Âliye (The Sublime State)
· Ottoman Turkish/Persian: Devlet-i Ebed-Müddet
· Ottoman Turkish/Persian: Memâlik-i Mahrûse (The Well-Protected Domains)
· Ottoman Turkish/Persian: Memâlik-i Mahrûse-i Osmanî
· Modern Turkish: OsmanlÄ± Ä°mparatorluÄŸu (Ottoman Empire),
· Arabic: Ø§Ù„Ø¯ÙˆÙ„Ø©Ù Ø§Ù„Ø¹Ù„ÙŠØ©Ù Ø§Ù„Ø¹Ø«Ù…Ø§Ù†ÙŠØ©Ù Ad-Dawlat al-Ë¤Ä€lÄ« al-Ë¤UthmÄ nÄ«
· Bulgarian: ÐžÑ Ð¼Ð°Ð½Ñ ÐºÐ° Ð¸Ð¼Ð¿ÐµÑ€Ð¸Ñ (Osmanska Imperia)
· Greek: ΟθωμανικÎ® ΑυτοκρατορÎ¯α
· Armenian: Õ•Õ½Õ´Õ¡Õ¶ÕµÕ¡Õ¶ Ô¿Õ¡ÕµÕ½Ö€Õ¸Ö‚Õ©ÕµÕ¸Ö‚Õ¶ (Osmanyan Kaysroutyoun)

In diplomatic circles, the Ottoman government was often referred to as the "Sublime Porte", a literal translation of the Ottoman Turkish Bâb-Ä± Âlî, which was the only gate of the imperial TopkapÄ± Palace that was open to foreigners, and where the Sultan, Grand Vizier or Viziers greeted the ambassadors.

Ottoman Turks

The Ottoman Turks were the subdivision of the Ottoman Muslim Millet that dominated the ruling class of the Ottoman Empire. Reliable information about the early history of the Ottomans is scarce. According to some sources (references needed), the leader (khan) of the Kayi tribe of the Oguz Turks, Ertugrul, left Persia in the mid-thirteenth century to escape the invading Mongols.

| | |
|---|---|
| Portugal | Portugal , officially the Portuguese Republic (Portuguese: República Portuguesa), is a country on the Iberian Peninsula, member of the European Union and one of the founding members of NATO. Located in southwestern Europe, Portugal is the westernmost country of mainland Europe and is bordered by the Atlantic Ocean to the west and south and by Spain to the north and east. The Atlantic archipelagos of the Azores and Madeira are also part of Portugal. The land within the borders of today"s Portuguese Republic has been continuously settled since prehistoric times. |
| Appeasement | Appeasement is "the policy of settling international quarrels by admitting and satisfying grievances through rational negotiation and compromise, thereby avoiding the resort to an armed conflict which would be expensive, bloody, and possibly dangerous." The term is most often applied to the foreign policy of British Prime Minister Neville Chamberlain towards Nazi Germany between 1937 and 1939. Appeasement has been the subject of debate for eighty years among academics and politicians. The historian"s assessment of Chamberlain has ranged from condemnation to the judgment that he had no alternative and acted in Britain"s best interests. |
| Revolution | A Revolution is a fundamental change in power or organizational structures that takes place in a relatively short period of time. Aristotle described two types of political Revolution<br><br>· Complete change from one constitution to another<br>· Modification of an existing constitution.<br>Revolution s have occurred through human history and vary widely in terms of methods, duration, and motivating ideology. |
| Empire | The term Empire derives from the Latin imperium. Politically, an Empire is a geographically extensive group of states and peoples united and ruled either by a monarch (emperor, empress) or an oligarchy. Geopolitically, the term Empire has denoted very different, territorially-extreme states -- at the strong end, the extensive Spanish Empire and the British Empire (19th c)., at the weak end, the Holy Roman Empire (8th c.-19th c)., in its Medieval and early-modern forms, and the Byzantine Empire (15th c)., that was a direct continuation of the Roman Empire, that, in its final century of existence, was more a city-state than a territorial Empire. |
| Pragmatic Sanction | A Pragmatic sanction is a sovereign"s solemn decree on a matter of primary importance and has the force of fundamental law. In the late history of the Holy Roman Empire it referred more specifically to an edict issued by the Emperor. When used as a proper noun, not otherwise qualified, it usually refers to the Pragmatic sanction of 1713, a legal mechanism designed to ensure that the Austrian throne and Habsburg lands would be inherited by Emperor Charles VI"s daughter, Maria Theresa. |
| Brandenburg-Prussia | Brandenburg-Prussia was a German monarchy established by the personal union between the Duchy of Prussia and the Margraviate of Brandenburg in 1618. |

| | |
|---|---|
| | The monarchy was ruled by the branch of the Hohenzollern dynasty that had earlier ruled Brandenburg. The term Brandenburg-Prussia refers to this monarchy from its establishment until 1701, after which it is usually known as the Kingdom of Prussia. |
| India | India, officially the Indian Empire, declared war on Germany in September 1939. The Provinces of India " href="/wiki/East_African_Campaign_(World_War_II)">East African Campaign, Western Desert Campaign and the Italian Campaign. At the height of the World War, more than 2.5 million Indian troops were fighting Axis forces around the globe. |
| Colony | In politics and in history, a Colony is a territory under the immediate political control of a state. For colonies in antiquity, city-states would often found their own colonies. Some colonies were historically countries, while others were territories without definite statehood from their inception. |
| Popular Front | A Popular Front is a broad coalition of different political groupings, often made up of leftists and centrists who are united by opposition to another group (most often capitalist groups). Being very broad, they can sometimes include centrist and liberal (or "bourgeois") forces as well as socialist and communist ("working-class") groups. Popular Fronts are larger in scope than united fronts, which contain only working-class groups. |
| Flying shuttle | The Flying shuttle was one of the key developments in weaving that helped fuel the Industrial Revolution. It was patented by John Kay (1704 - 1764) in 1733. In order to understand the importance of this invention, it is useful to review the action of weaving prior to it. |
| October | October Â·) is the tenth month of the year in the Gregorian Calendar and one of seven Gregorian months with a length of 31 days. The eighth month in the old Roman calendar, October retained its name when January and February were added. When the calendar was originally created by the Romans, the year began in March this meant that instead of October being the 10th month of the year it was originally the 8th month of the year. |
| Italy | Italy (Italian: Italia), officially the Italian Republic (Italian: Repubblica Italiana), is a country located on the Italian Peninsula in Southern Europe and on the two largest islands in the Mediterranean Sea, Sicily and Sardinia. Italy shares its northern, Alpine boundary with France, Switzerland, Austria and Slovenia. The independent states of San Marino and the Vatican City are enclaves within the Italian Peninsula, and Campione d"Italia is an Italian exclave in Switzerland. |

| | |
|---|---|
| Revolution | A Revolution is a fundamental change in power or organizational structures that takes place in a relatively short period of time. Aristotle described two types of political Revolution<br><br>· Complete change from one constitution to another<br>· Modification of an existing constitution.<br>Revolution s have occurred through human history and vary widely in terms of methods, duration, and motivating ideology. |
| Revolutionary | A Revolutionary is a person who either actively participates in, or advocates revolution. Also, when used as an adjective, the term Revolutionary refers to something that has a major, sudden impact on society or on some aspect of human endeavour. The term--both as a noun and adjective--is usually applied to the field of politics, and is occasionally used in the context of science, invention or art. |
| United States | The United States retained a fully civilian democratic government structure throughout World War II. Certain expediencies were taken within the existing structure of the Federal government, such as conscription and other violations of civil liberties, and the incarceration and later dispersal of Japanese-Americans. Still, elections were held as scheduled in 1944.<br>The United States entered World War II with the same Administration that had been at the helm of the nation since 1932, that of Franklin Delano Roosevelt. |
| Articles of Confederation | The Articles of Confederation and Perpetual Union, commonly referred to as the Articles of Confederation, was the first constitution of the thirteen United States of America and legally established the Union of the States. The Second Continental Congress appointed a committee to draft the "Articles" in June 1776 and proposed the draft to the States for ratification in November 1777. The ratification process was completed in March 1781, legally federating the sovereign and independent states, allied under the Articles of Association, into a new federation styled the "United States of America". |
| Constitution | A Constitution is set of rules for government--often codified as a written document--that establishes principles of an autonomous political entity. In the case of countries, this term refers specifically to a national Constitution defining the fundamental political principles, and establishing the structure, procedures, powers and duties, of a government. By limiting the government"s own reach, most Constitutions guarantee certain rights to the people. |
| Declaration of Independence | A Declaration of independence is an assertion of the independence of an aspiring state or states. Such places are usually declared from part or all of the territory of another nation or failed nation, or are breakaway territories from within the larger state. Not all declarations of independence were successful and resulted in independence for these regions. |
| France | France or ; French: [fɛ  ɛˈĺ ʃs]), officially the French Republic , is a country located in Western Europe, with several overseas islands and territories located on other continents. Metropolitan France extends from the Mediterranean Sea to the English Channel and the North Sea, and from the Rhine to the Atlantic Ocean. It is often referred to as L"Hexagone ("The Hexagon") because of the geometric shape of its territory. |

| | |
|---|---|
| Law | The great end, for which men entered into society, was to secure their property. That right is preserved sacred and incommunicable in all instances, where it has not been taken away or abridged by some public Law for the good of the whole ... If no excuse can be found or produced, the silence of the books is an authority against the defendant, and the plaintiff must have judgment. |
| Peasant | A Peasant is an agricultural worker who subsists by working a small plot of ground. The term Peasant today is sometimes used in a pejorative sense for impoverished farmers.<br><br>Peasants typically make up the majority of the agricultural labour force in a Pre-industrial society, dependent on the cultivation of their land: without stockpiles of provisions they thrive or starve according to the most recent harvest. |
| Estates-General | The Estates-General (or States-General) of 1789 was the first meeting since 1614 of the French Estates-General, a general assembly representing the French collection of peoples. The independence from the Crown which it displayed paved the way for the French Revolution.<br><br>Among the direct causes of the French Revolution was a massive financial crisis caused by France"s enormous national debt, the lack of food and its outrageous prices, the desire to imitate the American Revolution, the government"s lavish spending, and an archaic system of taxation which brought little money to the national coffers though placing the tax burden upon the Third Estate , while virtually ignoring the First Estate (the Clergy) and the Second Estate (the Nobility). |
| Popular Front | A Popular Front is a broad coalition of different political groupings, often made up of leftists and centrists who are united by opposition to another group (most often capitalist groups). Being very broad, they can sometimes include centrist and liberal (or "bourgeois") forces as well as socialist and communist ("working-class") groups. Popular Fronts are larger in scope than united fronts, which contain only working-class groups. |
| National Assembly | Foreign relations<br>Democracy movement in Nepal<br>Civil War |

Other countries Â· Atlas

Politics portal

| | |
|---|---|
| | The National Assembly (Nepali: Rashtriya Sabha) was the upper house of parliament in Nepal during the 1990 Constitution. It Nepal had 60 members, 10 nominated by the king, 35 elected by the House of Representatives and the remaining 15 elected by an electoral college made up of chairs of villages and towns. The legislature had a six-year term, and could be dissolved by the king. |
| National Convention | During the French Revolution, the National Convention or Convention, in France, comprised the constitutional and legislative assembly which sat from 20 September 1792 to 26 October 1795 . It held executive power in France during the first years of the French First Republic. It was succeeded by the Directory, commencing 2 November 1795. |

| | |
|---|---|
| Rebellion | Rebellion is a refusal of obedience. It may, therefore, be seen as encompassing a range of behaviors from civil disobedience and mass nonviolent resistance, to violent and organized attempts to destroy an established authority such as the government. Those who participate in Rebellions are known as "rebels". |
| Legislative Assembly | Legislative Assembly is the name given in some countries to either a legislature, or to one of its chambers. The name is used by a number of member-states of the Commonwealth of Nations, as well as in a number of Latin American countries.<br>A number of colonies in the British Empire were given a degree of involvement in running their own affairs by the creation of a representative body, often named the Legislative Assembly. |
| Austria | Austria ), officially the Republic of Austria , is a landlocked country of roughly 8.3 million people in Central Europe. It borders both Germany and the Czech Republic to the north, Slovakia and Hungary to the east, Slovenia and Italy to the south, and Switzerland and Liechtenstein to the west. The territory of Austria covers 83,872 square kilometres (32,383 sq mi), and is influenced by a temperate and alpine climate. |
| Mountain | A Mountain is a large landform that stretches above the surrounding land in a limited area usually in the form of a peak. A Mountain is generally steeper than a hill. The adjective montane is used to describe Mountainous areas and things associated with them. |
| Paris Commune | The Paris Commune was a government that briefly ruled Paris, from March 28 to May 28, 1871. It existed before the split between anarchists and socialists had taken place, and it is hailed by both groups as the first assumption of power by the working class. Debates over the policies and outcome of the Commune contributed to the break between those two political groups. |
| Reign of Terror | The Reign of Terror incited by conflict between rival political factions, the Girondins and the Jacobins, and marked by mass executions of "enemies of the revolution." Estimates vary widely as to how many were killed, with numbers ranging from 16,000 to 40,000; in many cases, records were not kept they are considered likely to be inaccurate. The guillotine became the symbol of a string of executions: Marie Antoinette, the Girondins Philippe Égalité and Madame Roland, as well as many others, such as "the father of modern chemistry" Antoine Lavoisier, lost their lives under its blade.<br>During 1794, revolutionary France was beset with real or imagined conspiracies by internal and foreign enemies. |
| Empire | The term Empire derives from the Latin imperium. Politically, an Empire is a geographically extensive group of states and peoples united and ruled either by a monarch (emperor, empress) or an oligarchy. Geopolitically, the term Empire has denoted very different, territorially-extreme states -- at the strong end, the extensive Spanish Empire and the British Empire (19th c.)., at the weak end, the Holy Roman Empire (8th c.-19th c)., in its Medieval and early-modern forms, and the Byzantine Empire (15th c.), that was a direct continuation of the Roman Empire, that, in its final century of existence, was more a city-state than a territorial Empire. |

| | |
|---|---|
| Ottoman | The state of the Ottomans which began as part of the Anatolian Seljuk Sultanate and became an independent Empire, has been known historically by different names at different periods and in various languages. This page surveys the history of these names and their usage.<br><br>· Modern Turkish: OsmanlÄ± BeyliÄŸi;<br>The first declaration of statehood happened under Osman I.<br><br>· Ä€l-e Uá¹mÄ n<br><br>· Medieval Latin: Turchia<br>· Medieval Latin: Imperium Turcicum<br>· English: Turkey ; the current use of the name Turkey refers to the Republic of Turkey which succeeded the Ottoman Empire in 1923<br>· English: Turkish Empire, Ottoman Empire, Osmanic Empire, Osmanian Empire<br>· Ottoman Turkish/Persian: Ø¯ÙˆÙ„Øª Ø¹Ù„ÙŠÚ‡ Ø¹Ø«Ù…Ø§Ù†ÙŠÚ‡ Devlet-i Âliye-yi Osmâniyye<br>· Ottoman Turkish/Persian: Devlet-i Âliye (The Sublime State)<br>· Ottoman Turkish/Persian: Devlet-i Ebed-Müddet<br>· Ottoman Turkish/Persian: Memâlik-i Mahrûse (The Well-Protected Domains)<br>· Ottoman Turkish/Persian: Memâlik-i Mahrûse-i Osmanî<br>· Modern Turkish: OsmanlÄ± Ä°mparatorluÄŸu (Ottoman Empire),<br>· Arabic: Ø§Ù„Ø¯ÙˆÙ„Ø© Ø§Ù„Ø¹ÙŠØ©Ù Ø§Ù„Ø¹Ø«Ù…Ø§Ù†ÙŠØ©Ù Ad-Dawlat al-Ë¤Ä€lÄ« al-Ë¤UthmÄ nÄ«<br>· Bulgarian: ÐžÑ Ð¼Ð°Ð½Ñ ÐºÐ° Ð˜Ð¼Ð¿ÐµÑ€Ð¸Ñ (Osmanska Imperia)<br>· Greek: ÎŸθωμανικÎ® Αυτοκρατορία (Osmanyan Kaysroutyoun)<br>· Armenian: Õ•Õ½Õ´Õ¡Õ¶Õ¥Õ¡Õ¶ Õ¿Õ¡Õ¥Õ½Õ¸Ö‚Õ©Õ«Ö‚Õ¶ (Osmanyan Kaysroutyoun)<br>In diplomatic circles, the Ottoman government was often referred to as the "Sublime Porte", a literal translation of the Ottoman Turkish Bâb-Ä± Âlî, which was the only gate of the imperial TopkapÄ± Palace that was open to foreigners, and where the Sultan, Grand Vizier or Viziers greeted the ambassadors. |
| Ottoman Empire | The Ottoman Empire or Ottoman State , also known by its contemporaries as the Turkish Empire or Turkey , was an empire that lasted from 1299 to November 1, 1922 (as an imperial monarchy) or July 24, 1923 (de jure, as a state.) It was succeeded by the Republic of Turkey, which was officially proclaimed on October 29, 1923.<br>At the height of its power (16th-17th century), it spanned three continents, controlling much of Southeastern Europe, Western Asia and North Africa. |
| Slavery | Slavery (Romanian: robie) existed on the territory of present-day Romania from before the founding of the principalities of Wallachia and Moldavia in 13th-14th century, until it was abolished in stages during the 1840s and 1850s. Most of the slaves were of Roma (Gypsy) ethnicity. Particularly in Moldavia there were also slaves of Tatar ethnicity, probably prisoners captured from the wars with the Nogai and Crimean Tatars. |

| | |
|---|---|
| Napoleon Bonaparte | The ascendancy of Napoleon Bonaparte proved to be an important event in European Jewish emancipation from old laws restricting them to Jewish ghettos, as well as the many laws that limited Jews" rights to property, worship, and careers. |
| | The French Revolution abolished the different treatment of people according to religion or origin that existed under the monarchy; the 1789 Declaration of the Rights of Man and of the Citizen guaranteed freedom of religion and free exercise of worship, provided that it did not contradict public order. At that time, most other European countries implemented measures restricting the rights of people from minority religions. |
| Austrian Empire | The Austrian Empire was a modern era successor empire founded on a remnant of the Holy Roman Empire centered on what is today"s Austria that officially lasted from 1804 to 1867. It was followed by combining the Royal House with that of Hungary creating the dual monarchy Austria-Hungary , which itself as one of the losers was dissolved at the end of World War I and broken into separate new states). The term "Austrian Empire" is also used for the Habsburg possessions before 1804, which had no official collective name, although Austria is more frequent; the term of Austria-Hungary has also been used, incorrectly. |
| Austria-Hungary | Austria-Hungary the Dual Monarchy or the k.u.k Monarchy, was a state in Central Europe ruled by the House of Habsburg, constitutionally a monarchic union between the crowns of the Austrian Empire and the Kingdom of Hungary. The state was a result of the Ausgleich or Compromise of 1867, under which the Austrian Habsburgs agreed to share power with a separate Hungarian government, dividing the territory of the former Austrian Empire between them. The Dual Monarchy existed for 51 years until 1918, when it dissolved following military defeat in the First World War. |
| Alexander | Alexander was tagus or despot of Pherae in Thessaly, and ruled from 369 BC to 358 BC. |
| | The accounts of his usurpation vary somewhat in minor points. Diodorus Siculus tells us that on the assassination of his father, the tyrant Jason of Pherae, in 370 BC, his brother Polydorus ruled for a year, and was then poisoned by Alexander, another brother. According to Xenophon, Polydorus was murdered by his brother Polyphron, and Polyphron, in 369 BC murdered by Alexander--his nephew, according to Plutarch, who relates also that Alexander worshiped the spear with which he slew his uncle as if it was a god. |
| Coalition | A Coalition is an alliance among individuals or groups, during which they cooperate in joint action, each in his own self-interest, joining forces together for a common cause. This alliance may be temporary or a matter of convenience. A Coalition thus differs from a more formal covenant. |
| Ulm | Ulm is a city in the German Bundesland of Baden-Württemberg, situated on the River Danube. The city, whose population is estimated at 120,000 , forms an urban district of its own and is the administrative seat of the Alb-Donau district. Ulm founded around 850, is rich in history and traditions as a former Free Imperial City . |

| | |
|---|---|
| Colonization | Colonization, , occurs whenever any one or more species populate an area. The term, which is derived from the Latin colere, "to inhabit, cultivate, frequent, practice, tend, guard, respect," originally related to humans. However, 19th century biogeographers dominated the term to describe the activities of birds, bacteria, or plant species. |
| Liberal Party | Liberal Party is the name of dozens of political parties around the world. It usually designates a party that is ideologically liberal, meaning that they advocate individual rights and civil liberties, and sometimes left wing, meaning that they are reliant on governmental solutions to social and economic problems. There are also some Liberal Parties which subscribe to classical liberalism and therefore support a mostly unregulated free market. |
| May | May Â·) is the fifth month of the year in the Gregorian Calendar and one of seven Gregorian months with the length of 31 days. It is also a month within the northern season of spring.<br>The month May has been named for the Greek goddess Maia, who was identified with the Roman era goddess of fertility, Bona Dea, whose festival was held in May. |

Capital |

| Flag

The three occupation zones. Blue indicates the Italian, red the German and green the Bulgarian zones. The Italian zone was taken over by the Germans in September 1943.

Capital                   Athens

Political structure      Puppet state

Prime Minister

- 1941-1942              Georgios Tsolakoglou

- 1942-1943              Konst.

Industrial Revolution

The Industrial Revolution was a period in the late 18th and early 19th centuries where major changes in agriculture, manufacturing, mining, and transport had a profound effect on the socioeconomic and cultural conditions in the United Kingdom. The changes subsequently spread throughout Europe, North America, and eventually the world. The onset of the Industrial Revolution marked a major turning point in human society; almost every aspect of daily life was eventually influenced in some way.

Revolution

A Revolution is a fundamental change in power or organizational structures that takes place in a relatively short period of time. Aristotle described two types of political Revolution

· Complete change from one constitution to another
· Modification of an existing constitution.

Revolution s have occurred through human history and vary widely in terms of methods, duration, and motivating ideology.

France

France or ; French: [fÉ› É›ìfs]), officially the French Republic , is a country located in Western Europe, with several overseas islands and territories located on other continents. Metropolitan France extends from the Mediterranean Sea to the English Channel and the North Sea, and from the Rhine to the Atlantic Ocean. It is often referred to as L"Hexagone ("The Hexagon") because of the geometric shape of its territory.

History

Regions

Larger cities

Smaller cities

Major Towns

Counties

Flying shuttle

The Flying shuttle was one of the key developments in weaving that helped fuel the Industrial Revolution. It was patented by John Kay (1704 - 1764) in 1733.
In order to understand the importance of this invention, it is useful to review the action of weaving prior to it.

Power loom

The first Power loom, a mechanized loom powered by a drive shaft, was designed in 1784 by Edmund Cartwright and first built in 1785, it was refined over the next 47 years till a design by Kenworthy and Bullough, made the operation completely automatic. This was known as the Lancashire Loom By 1850 there were 250,000 machines in operation in England. Fifty years later came the Northrop Loom that would replenish the shuttle when it was empty and this replaced the Lancashire loom.

Spinning jenny

The Spinning jenny is a multi-spool spinning wheel. It was invented c. 1764 by James Hargreaves in Stanhill, near Blackburn, Lancashire in the northwest of England.

Force

In physics, a Force is any external agent that causes a change in the motion of a free body, or that causes stress in a fixed body. It can also be described by intuitive concepts such as a push or pull that can cause an object with mass to change its velocity , i.e., to accelerate, or which can cause a flexible object to deform. Force has both magnitude and direction, making it a vector quantity.

Factory

A Factory (previously manuFactory) or manufacturing plant is an industrial building where workers manufacture goods or supervise machines processing one product into another. Most modern factories have large warehouses or warehouse-like facilities that contain heavy equipment used for assembly line production. Typically, factories gather and concentrate resources: workers, capital and plant.

| Green Party | A Green Party or ecologist party is a formally organized political party based on the principles of Green politics. These principles include environmentalism, reliance on grassroots democracy, nonviolence, and support for social justice causes, including those related to the rights of indigenous peoples, among others. "Greens" believe that the exercise of these principles leads to the health of people, societies, and ecosystems. |
|---|---|
| Nazi Germany | Nazi Germany and the Third Reich are the common English names for Germany between 1933 and 1945, while it was led by Adolf Hitler and the National Socialist German Worker"s Party . The name Third Reich (Drittes Reich, "Third Reich") refers to the state as the successor to the Holy Roman Empire of the Middle Ages and the German Empire of 1871-1918. In German, the state was known as Deutsches Reich until 1943, when its official name became Großdeutsches Reich . |
| Massachusetts | The Commonwealth of Massachusetts () is a state in the New England region of the northeastern United States. It is bordered by Rhode Island and Connecticut to the south, New York to the west, and Vermont and New Hampshire to the north; at its east lies the Atlantic Ocean. Most of its population of 6.4 million lives in the Boston metropolitan area. |
| Mill town | A Mill town is typically a settlement that developed around one or more mills or factories. Oldham in Greater Manchester, England is an archetypal British "Mill town". Although its textile producing days are over, it is still home to many historic cotton mills. <br> In the United Kingdom, the term "Mill town" often refers to the 19th century textile-manufacturing towns of northern England and the Scottish Lowlands, particularly those in Lancashire and Yorkshire. |
| Congress | The 2001 Congress of the Greens/Green Party USA, held at Carbondale, Illinois, was a critical event in the history of the Green Party in the United States. At the Congress, occurring July 20 to July 23, at which the G/GPUSA was to consider the Boston Proposal , a tentative "merger" agreement between it and the Association of State Green Parties (ASGP). After an intense internal organizational struggle, most of which revolved around whether or not to "accredit" various delegations (and thus grant the individuals within them voting privileges), the proposal was rejected; although 55% of the members in attendance voted to approve it (99 in favor, 81 against), the organization"s bylaws required yes votes from a "super-majority" of 66.7% of the delegates in attendance to pass. |
| India | India, officially the Indian Empire, declared war on Germany in September 1939. The Provinces of India " href="/wiki/East_African_Campaign_(World_War_II)">East African Campaign, Western Desert Campaign and the Italian Campaign. At the height of the World War, more than 2.5 million Indian troops were fighting Axis forces around the globe. |
| Indian National Congress | From its foundation on 28 December 1885 till the time of independence of India on August 15, 1947, the Indian National Congress was the largest and most prominent Indian public organization, and central and defining influence of the Indian Independence Movement. <br> Although initially and primarily a political body, the Congress transformed itself into a national vehicle for social reform and human upliftment. And the Congress"s foundations in democracy and multiculturalism helped make India a consistently democratic and free nation. |

| Rebellion | Rebellion is a refusal of obedience. It may, therefore, be seen as encompassing a range of behaviors from civil disobedience and mass nonviolent resistance, to violent and organized attempts to destroy an established authority such as the government. Those who participate in Rebellions are known as "rebels". |
|---|---|
| Law | The great end, for which men entered into society, was to secure their property. That right is preserved sacred and incommunicable in all instances, where it has not been taken away or abridged by some public Law for the good of the whole ... If no excuse can be found or produced, the silence of the books is an authority against the defendant, and the plaintiff must have judgment. |
| Charter | A Charter is the grant of authority or rights, stating that the granter formally recognizes the prerogative of the recipient to exercise the rights specified. It is implicit that the granter retains superiority (or sovereignty), and that the recipient admits a limited (or inferior) status within the relationship, and it is within that sense that Charters were historically granted, and that sense is retained in modern usage of the term. Also, Charter can simply be a document giving royal permission to start a colony. |
| Luddite | The Luddites were a social movement of British textile artisans in the early nineteenth century who protested--often by destroying mechanized looms--against the changes produced by the Industrial Revolution, which they felt were leaving them without work and changing their entire way of life. This English historical movement should be seen in the context of the era"s harsh economic climate due to the Napoleonic Wars, and the degrading working conditions in the new textile factories. Since then, however, the term Luddite has been used derisively to describe anyone opposed to technological progress and technological change. |

Congress

The 2001 Congress of the Greens/Green Party USA, held at Carbondale, Illinois, was a critical event in the history of the Green Party in the United States. At the Congress, occurring July 20 to July 23, at which the G/GPUSA was to consider the Boston Proposal , a tentative "merger" agreement between it and the Association of State Green Parties (ASGP). After an intense internal organizational struggle, most of which revolved around whether or not to "accredit" various delegations (and thus grant the individuals within them voting privileges), the proposal was rejected; although 55% of the members in attendance voted to approve it (99 in favor, 81 against), the organization"s bylaws required yes votes from a "super-majority" of 66.7% of the delegates in attendance to pass.

Austrian Empire

The Austrian Empire was a modern era successor empire founded on a remnant of the Holy Roman Empire centered on what is today"s Austria that officially lasted from 1804 to 1867. It was followed by combining the Royal House with that of Hungary creating the dual monarchy Austria-Hungary , which itself as one of the losers was dissolved at the end of World War I and broken into separate new states). The term "Austrian Empire" is also used for the Habsburg possessions before 1804, which had no official collective name, although Austria is more frequent; the term of Austria-Hungary has also been used, incorrectly.

Appeasement

Appeasement is "the policy of settling international quarrels by admitting and satisfying grievances through rational negotiation and compromise, thereby avoiding the resort to an armed conflict which would be expensive, bloody, and possibly dangerous." The term is most often applied to the foreign policy of British Prime Minister Neville Chamberlain towards Nazi Germany between 1937 and 1939. Appeasement has been the subject of debate for eighty years among academics and politicians. The historian"s assessment of Chamberlain has ranged from condemnation to the judgment that he had no alternative and acted in Britain"s best interests.

France

France or ; French: [fɛ Éˈ̍ʃfs]), officially the French Republic , is a country located in Western Europe, with several overseas islands and territories located on other continents. Metropolitan France extends from the Mediterranean Sea to the English Channel and the North Sea, and from the Rhine to the Atlantic Ocean. It is often referred to as L"Hexagone ("The Hexagon") because of the geometric shape of its territory.

Revolution

A Revolution is a fundamental change in power or organizational structures that takes place in a relatively short period of time. Aristotle described two types of political Revolution

· Complete change from one constitution to another
· Modification of an existing constitution.
Revolution s have occurred through human history and vary widely in terms of methods, duration, and motivating ideology.

Argentina

Argentina, officially the Argentine Republic , is the second largest country in South America, constituted as a federation of 23 provinces and an autonomous city, Buenos Aires. It is the eighth largest country in the world by land area and the largest among Spanish-speaking nations, though Mexico, Colombia and Spain are more populous. Its continental area is between the Andes mountain range in the west and the Atlantic Ocean in the east.

| | |
|---|---|
| Italy | Italy (Italian: Italia), officially the Italian Republic (Italian: Repubblica Italiana), is a country located on the Italian Peninsula in Southern Europe and on the two largest islands in the Mediterranean Sea, Sicily and Sardinia. Italy shares its northern, Alpine boundary with France, Switzerland, Austria and Slovenia. The independent states of San Marino and the Vatican City are enclaves within the Italian Peninsula, and Campione d"Italia is an Italian exclave in Switzerland. |
| Peru | Peru , officially the Republic of Peru ), is a country in western South America. It is bordered on the north by Ecuador and Colombia, on the east by Brazil, on the southeast by Bolivia, on the south by Chile, and on the west by the Pacific Ocean. <br> Peruvian territory was home to the Norte Chico civilization, one of the oldest in the world, and to the Inca Empire, the largest state in Pre-Columbian America. The Spanish Empire conquered the region in the 16th century and established a Viceroyalty, which included most of its South American colonies. After achieving independence in 1821, Peru has undergone periods of political unrest and fiscal crisis as well as periods of stability and economic upswing. |
| Venezuela | Venezuela , officially titled Bolivarian Republic of Venezuela , is a tropical country on the northern coast of South America. It is a continental mainland with numerous islands located off its coastline in the Caribbean Sea. <br> Venezuela possesses recognized borders with Guyana to the east of the Essequibo river, Brazil to the south, and Colombia to the west. Trinidad and Tobago, Grenada, St. Lucia, Barbados, Curaçao, Bonaire, Aruba, Saint Vincent and the Grenadines and the Leeward Antilles lie just north, off the Venezuelan coast. |
| Greece | Greece entered World War II on 28 October 1940, when the Italian army invaded from Albania. The Greek army dealt the first victory for the Allies by defeating the invasion and pushing Mussolini"s forces back into Albania. Hitler was reluctantly forced to send his own forces to overcome Greece in April 1941, and delay the invasion of the Soviet Union by six weeks. |
| Koinon | The Koinon (or "League") of Free Laconians was established in 21 BC by the Emperor Augustus, giving formal structure to a group of cities that had been associated for almost two centuries. <br> The Eleutherolakones (á¼˜λευθερολÎ¬κωνες, free Laconians) are first mentioned in 195 BC, after Sparta"s defeat in the Roman-Spartan War. The Roman general Titus Quinctius Flaminius placed several coastal cities of the Mani Peninsula under the protection of the Achean League, freeing them from Spartan hegemony. |
| Moldavia | Moldavia is a geographic and historical region and former principality in Eastern Europe, corresponding to the territory between the Eastern Carpathians and the Dniester river. An initially independent and later autonomous state, it existed from the 14th century to 1859, when it united with Wallachia as the basis of the modern Romanian state; at various times, the state included the regions of Bessarabia and all of Bukovina. The western part of Moldavia is now part of Romania and the eastern part belongs to the Republic of Moldova, while the northern and south-eastern parts are territories of Ukraine. |

| | |
|---|---|
| Ottoman | The state of the Ottomans which began as part of the Anatolian Seljuk Sultanate and became an independent Empire, has been known historically by different names at different periods and in various languages. This page surveys the history of these names and their usage.<br><br>· Modern Turkish: OsmanlÄ± BeyliÄŸi;<br>The first declaration of statehood happened under Osman I.<br><br>· Ä€l-e Uá'mÄ n<br><br>· Medieval Latin: Turchia<br>· Medieval Latin: Imperium Turcicum<br>· English: Turkey ; the current use of the name Turkey refers to the Republic of Turkey which succeeded the Ottoman Empire in 1923<br>· English: Turkish Empire, Ottoman Empire, Osmanic Empire, Osmanian Empire<br>· Ottoman Turkish/Persian: Ø¯Ù˜Ù„Øª Ø¹Ù„ÙŠÙ‡ Ø¹Ø«Ù…Ø§Ù†ÙŠÙ‡ Devlet-i Âliye-yi Osmâniyye<br>· Ottoman Turkish/Persian: Devlet-i Âliye (The Sublime State)<br>· Ottoman Turkish/Persian: Devlet-i Ebed-Müddet<br>· Ottoman Turkish/Persian: Memâlik-i Mahrûse (The Well-Protected Domains)<br>· Ottoman Turkish/Persian: Memâlik-i Mahrûse-i Osmanî<br>· Modern Turkish: OsmanlÄ± Ä°mparatorluÄŸu (Ottoman Empire),<br>· Arabic: Ø§Ù„Ø¯ÙˆÙ„Ø©  Ø§Ù„Ø¹Ù„ÙŠØ©  Ø§Ù„Ø«Ù…Ø§Ù†ÙŠØ©  Ad-Dawlat al-ˤĀlÄ« al-ˤUthmÄ nÄ«<br>· Bulgarian: ÐžÑ Ð¼Ð°Ð½Ñ Ð°Ð° Ð˜Ð¼Ð¿ÐµÑ€Ð¸Ñ  (Osmanska Imperia)<br>· Greek: ÎŸÎ¸Ï‰Î¼Î±Î½Î¹ÎºÎ® Î'Ï…Ï„Î¿ÎºÏ Î±Ï„Î¿Ï Î¯Î±<br>· Armenian: Õ•Õ½Õ´Õ¡Õ¶ÕµÕ¡Õ¶ Ô¿Õ¡ÕµÕ½Ö€Õ¸Ö‚Õ©ÕµÕ¸Ö‚Õ¶ (Osmanyan Kaysroutyoun)<br>In diplomatic circles, the Ottoman government was often referred to as the "Sublime Porte", a literal translation of the Ottoman Turkish Bâb-Ä± Âlî, which was the only gate of the imperial TopkapÄ± Palace that was open to foreigners, and where the Sultan, Grand Vizier or Viziers greeted the ambassadors. |
| Ottoman Empire | The Ottoman Empire or Ottoman State , also known by its contemporaries as the Turkish Empire or Turkey , was an empire that lasted from 1299 to November 1, 1922 (as an imperial monarchy) or July 24, 1923 (de jure, as a state.) It was succeeded by the Republic of Turkey, which was officially proclaimed on October 29, 1923.<br>At the height of its power (16th-17th century), it spanned three continents, controlling much of Southeastern Europe, Western Asia and North Africa. |
| Law | The great end, for which men entered into society, was to secure their property. That right is preserved sacred and incommunicable in all instances, where it has not been taken away or abridged by some public Law for the good of the whole ... If no excuse can be found or produced, the silence of the books is an authority against the defendant, and the plaintiff must have judgment. |

| | |
|---|---|
| Popular Front | A Popular Front is a broad coalition of different political groupings, often made up of leftists and centrists who are united by opposition to another group (most often capitalist groups). Being very broad, they can sometimes include centrist and liberal (or "bourgeois") forces as well as socialist and communist ("working-class") groups. Popular Fronts are larger in scope than united fronts, which contain only working-class groups. |
| Alexander | Alexander was tagus or despot of Pherae in Thessaly, and ruled from 369 BC to 358 BC. <br> The accounts of his usurpation vary somewhat in minor points. Diodorus Siculus tells us that on the assassination of his father, the tyrant Jason of Pherae, in 370 BC, his brother Polydorus ruled for a year, and was then poisoned by Alexander, another brother. According to Xenophon, Polydorus was murdered by his brother Polyphron, and Polyphron, in 369 BC murdered by Alexander--his nephew, according to Plutarch, who relates also that Alexander worshiped the spear with which he slew his uncle as if it was a god. |
| Michael | Michael is a given name that comes from the Hebrew: žÖ´×™×›Ö¸× Öµ×œ / ×ž×™×™×× ×œ×â€Ž , meaning "Who is like God?" In English, it is sometimes shortened to Mike, Mikey, or, especially in Ireland, Mick. <br> Michael is one of the Archangels. <br> Female forms of Michael include Michele, Michelle, Michaela, Mechelle, Micheline, and Michaelle, although there are women with the name Michael, such as Michael Learned. |
| Tsar | Tsar or czar , Ukrainian: Ñ†Ð°Ñ€, in Serbian: Ñ†Ð°Ñ€ / car, in scientific transliteration respectively car" and car), occasionally spelled csar or tzar in English, is a Slavic term with Bulgarian origins used to designate certain monarchs. The first ruler to adopt the title Tsar was Simeon I of Bulgaria <br> Originally, the title Czar " href="/wiki/Caesar_(title)">Caesar) meant Emperor in the European medieval sense of the term, that is, a ruler who claims the same rank as a Roman emperor, with the approval of another emperor or a supreme ecclesiastical official (the Pope or the Ecumenical Patriarch). <br> Occasionally, the word could be used to designate other, non-Christian, supreme rulers. |
| Austria-Hungary | Austria-Hungary the Dual Monarchy or the k.u.k Monarchy, was a state in Central Europe ruled by the House of Habsburg, constitutionally a monarchic union between the crowns of the Austrian Empire and the Kingdom of Hungary. The state was a result of the Ausgleich or Compromise of 1867, under which the Austrian Habsburgs agreed to share power with a separate Hungarian government, dividing the territory of the former Austrian Empire between them. The Dual Monarchy existed for 51 years until 1918, when it dissolved following military defeat in the First World War. |
| Liberalism | This article gives information on liberalism in diverse countries around the world. It is an overview of parties that adhere more or less (explicitly) to the ideas of political liberalism and is therefore a list of liberal parties around the world. <br> One can argue what a liberal party is. |

| African Americans | Due to the prevailing social climate that existed in the United States after World War II, one in which racism was a prominent factor, African Americans did not benefit from the provisions of the G. I. Bill of Rights as much as their white counterparts. Though the bill did provide a more level playing field than the one blacks faced during Reconstruction, this is not saying much. Representative John Elliott Rankin, an economic liberal who was also an avid segregationalist and racist, sponsored the bill in the United States House of Representatives. |
|---|---|
| July | July Â·) is the seventh month of the year in the Gregorian Calendar and one of seven Gregorian months with the length of 31 days. It is, on average, the warmest month in most of the Northern hemisphere (where it is the second month of summer) and the coldest month in much of the Southern hemisphere. The second half of the year commences in July. |
| Oireachtas | From 1922 to 1937 the Oireachtas was the legislature of the Irish Free State. Until the final days of the Irish Free State it consisted of the King and two houses: Dáil Éireann and Seanad Éireann (also known as the "Senate").<br>Like the modern Oireachtas, the Free State legislature was dominated by the powerful, directly elected Dáil. |
| Republic | A Republic is a form of government in which the head of state is not a monarch and the people (or at least a part of its people) have an impact on its government. The word "Republic" is derived from the Latin phrase res publica which can be translated as "public affairs".<br>Both modern and ancient Republics vary widely in their ideology and composition. |
| Rebellion | Rebellion is a refusal of obedience. It may, therefore, be seen as encompassing a range of behaviors from civil disobedience and mass nonviolent resistance, to violent and organized attempts to destroy an established authority such as the government. Those who participate in Rebellions are known as "rebels". |
| Constitution | A Constitution is set of rules for government--often codified as a written document--that establishes principles of an autonomous political entity. In the case of countries, this term refers specifically to a national Constitution defining the fundamental political principles, and establishing the structure, procedures, powers and duties, of a government. By limiting the government"s own reach, most Constitutions guarantee certain rights to the people. |
| Party | A Party is a gathering of people who have been invited by a host for the purposes of socializing, conversation, and recreation. A Party will typically feature food and beverages, and often music and dancing as well.<br>Some parties are held in honor of a specific person, day, or event (e.g., a birthday Party, a Super Bowl Party, or a St. Patrick"s Day Party). |

Force

In physics, a Force is any external agent that causes a change in the motion of a free body, or that causes stress in a fixed body. It can also be described by intuitive concepts such as a push or pull that can cause an object with mass to change its velocity , i.e., to accelerate, or which can cause a flexible object to deform. Force has both magnitude and direction, making it a vector quantity.

Schutzmannschaft

Schutzmannschaft (abbr. Schuma) or Hilfspolizei (abbr. Hipo) were the collaborationist auxiliary police battalions of native policemen in occupied countries, which were created to fight the resistance during World War II mostly in the Eastern European countries occupied by Nazi Germany.

Liberal Party

Liberal Party is the name of dozens of political parties around the world. It usually designates a party that is ideologically liberal, meaning that they advocate individual rights and civil liberties, and sometimes left wing, meaning that they are reliant on governmental solutions to social and economic problems. There are also some Liberal Parties which subscribe to classical liberalism and therefore support a mostly unregulated free market.

| | |
|---|---|
| Empire | The term Empire derives from the Latin imperium. Politically, an Empire is a geographically extensive group of states and peoples united and ruled either by a monarch (emperor, empress) or an oligarchy. Geopolitically, the term Empire has denoted very different, territorially-extreme states -- at the strong end, the extensive Spanish Empire and the British Empire (19th c)., at the weak end, the Holy Roman Empire (8th c.-19th c)., in its Medieval and early-modern forms, and the Byzantine Empire (15th c)., that was a direct continuation of the Roman Empire, that, in its final century of existence, was more a city-state than a territorial Empire. |
| France | France or ; French: [fɛ Éˈìʃs]), officially the French Republic , is a country located in Western Europe, with several overseas islands and territories located on other continents. Metropolitan France extends from the Mediterranean Sea to the English Channel and the North Sea, and from the Rhine to the Atlantic Ocean. It is often referred to as L"Hexagone ("The Hexagon") because of the geometric shape of its territory. |
| Greece | Greece entered World War II on 28 October 1940, when the Italian army invaded from Albania. The Greek army dealt the first victory for the Allies by defeating the invasion and pushing Mussolini"s forces back into Albania. Hitler was reluctantly forced to send his own forces to overcome Greece in April 1941, and delay the invasion of the Soviet Union by six weeks. |
| Koinon | The Koinon (or "League") of Free Laconians was established in 21 BC by the Emperor Augustus, giving formal structure to a group of cities that had been associated for almost two centuries. The Eleutherolakones (á¼˜λευθερολÎ¬κωνες, free Laconians) are first mentioned in 195 BC, after Sparta"s defeat in the Roman-Spartan War. The Roman general Titus Quinctius Flaminius placed several coastal cities of the Mani Peninsula under the protection of the Achean League, freeing them from Spartan hegemony. |
| Moldavia | Moldavia is a geographic and historical region and former principality in Eastern Europe, corresponding to the territory between the Eastern Carpathians and the Dniester river. An initially independent and later autonomous state, it existed from the 14th century to 1859, when it united with Wallachia as the basis of the modern Romanian state; at various times, the state included the regions of Bessarabia and all of Bukovina. The western part of Moldavia is now part of Romania and the eastern part belongs to the Republic of Moldova, while the northern and south-eastern parts are territories of Ukraine. |
| Ottoman | The state of the Ottomans which began as part of the Anatolian Seljuk Sultanate and became an independent Empire, has been known historically by different names at different periods and in various languages. This page surveys the history of these names and their usage.<br><br>· Modern Turkish: OsmanlÄ± BeyliÄŸi;<br>The first declaration of statehood happened under Osman I.<br><br>· Ä€l-e Uá¹mÄ n |

· Medieval Latin: Turchia
· Medieval Latin: Imperium Turcicum
· English: Turkey ; the current use of the name Turkey refers to the Republic of Turkey which succeeded the Ottoman Empire in 1923
· English: Turkish Empire, Ottoman Empire, Osmanic Empire, Osmanian Empire
· Ottoman Turkish/Persian: Ø¯ÙˆÙ„Øª Ø¹Ù„ÙŠÙ‡ Ø¹Ø«Ù…Ø§Ù†ÙŠÙ‡ Devlet-i Âliye-yi Osmâniyye
· Ottoman Turkish/Persian: Devlet-i Âliye (The Sublime State)
· Ottoman Turkish/Persian: Devlet-i Ebed-Müddet
· Ottoman Turkish/Persian: Memâlik-i Mahrûse (The Well-Protected Domains)
· Ottoman Turkish/Persian: Memâlik-i Mahrûse-i Osmanî
· Modern Turkish: OsmanlÄ± Ä°mparatorluÄŸu (Ottoman Empire),
· Arabic: Ø§Ù„Ø¯ÙˆÙ„Ø©Ù Ø§Ù„Ø¹Ù„ÙŠØ©Ù Ø§Ù„Ø¹Ø«Ù…Ø§Ù†ÙŠØ©Ù Ad-Dawlat al-Ë¤Ä€lÄ« al-Ë¤UthmÄ nÄ«
· Bulgarian: ÐžÑ Ð¼Ð°Ð½Ñ ÐºÐ° Ð¸Ð¼Ð¿ÐµÑ€Ð¸Ñ (Osmanska Imperia)
· Greek: ΟθωμανικÎ® ΑυτοκρατορÎ¯α
· Armenian: Õ•Õ½Õ´Õ¡Õ¶ÕµÕ¡Õ¶ Ô¿Õ¡ÕµÕ½Ö€Õ¸Ö‚Õ©ÕµÕ¸Ö‚Õ¶ (Osmanyan Kaysroutyoun)

In diplomatic circles, the Ottoman government was often referred to as the "Sublime Porte", a literal translation of the Ottoman Turkish Bâb-Ä± Âlî, which was the only gate of the imperial TopkapÄ± Palace that was open to foreigners, and where the Sultan, Grand Vizier or Viziers greeted the ambassadors.

Ottoman Empire

The Ottoman Empire or Ottoman State , also known by its contemporaries as the Turkish Empire or Turkey , was an empire that lasted from 1299 to November 1, 1922 (as an imperial monarchy) or July 24, 1923 (de jure, as a state.) It was succeeded by the Republic of Turkey, which was officially proclaimed on October 29, 1923.

At the height of its power (16th-17th century), it spanned three continents, controlling much of Southeastern Europe, Western Asia and North Africa.

Serbia

Serbia (Serbian: Ð¡Ñ€Ð±Ð¸Ñ˜Ð°, Srbija), officially the Republic of Serbia (Serbian: Ð ÐµÐ¿ÑƒÐ±Ð»Ð¸ÐºÐ° Ð¡Ñ€Ð±Ð¸Ñ˜Ð°, Republika Srbija), is a country located in both Central and Southeastern Europe. Its territory covers the southern part of the Pannonian Plain and central part of the Balkans. Serbia borders Hungary to the north; Romania and Bulgaria to the east; the Republic of Macedonia to the south; and Croatia, Bosnia and Herzegovina and Montenegro to the west.

Alexander

Alexander was tagus or despot of Pherae in Thessaly, and ruled from 369 BC to 358 BC.
The accounts of his usurpation vary somewhat in minor points. Diodorus Siculus tells us that on the assassination of his father, the tyrant Jason of Pherae, in 370 BC, his brother Polydorus ruled for a year, and was then poisoned by Alexander, another brother. According to Xenophon, Polydorus was murdered by his brother Polyphron, and Polyphron, in 369 BC murdered by Alexander--his nephew, according to Plutarch, who relates also that Alexander worshiped the spear with which he slew his uncle as if it was a god.

| | |
|---|---|
| Austrian Empire | The Austrian Empire was a modern era successor empire founded on a remnant of the Holy Roman Empire centered on what is today"s Austria that officially lasted from 1804 to 1867. It was followed by combining the Royal House with that of Hungary creating the dual monarchy Austria-Hungary , which itself as one of the losers was dissolved at the end of World War I and broken into separate new states). The term "Austrian Empire" is also used for the Habsburg possessions before 1804, which had no official collective name, although Austria is more frequent; the term of Austria-Hungary has also been used, incorrectly. |
| Italy | Italy (Italian: Italia), officially the Italian Republic (Italian: Repubblica Italiana), is a country located on the Italian Peninsula in Southern Europe and on the two largest islands in the Mediterranean Sea, Sicily and Sardinia. Italy shares its northern, Alpine boundary with France, Switzerland, Austria and Slovenia. The independent states of San Marino and the Vatican City are enclaves within the Italian Peninsula, and Campione d"Italia is an Italian exclave in Switzerland. |
| Rome | Rome is the capital of Italy and the country"s largest and most populous city, with over 2.7 million residents in a municipality of some 1,285.3 km$^2$ (496.3 sq mi), while the population of the urban area is estimated by Eurostat to be 3.46 million. The metropolitan area of Rome is estimated by OECD to have a population of 3.7 million. It is located in the central-western portion of the Italian Peninsula, on the Tiber river. |
| Austria | Austria ), officially the Republic of Austria , is a landlocked country of roughly 8.3 million people in Central Europe. It borders both Germany and the Czech Republic to the north, Slovakia and Hungary to the east, Slovenia and Italy to the south, and Switzerland and Liechtenstein to the west. The territory of Austria covers 83,872 square kilometres (32,383 sq mi), and is influenced by a temperate and alpine climate. |
| German Confederation | The German Confederation was the association of Central European states created by the Congress of Vienna in 1815 to serve as the successor to the Holy Roman Empire of the German Nation, which had been abolished in 1806. In 1848, revolutions by liberals and nationalists occurred in an attempt to establish a unified German state. Talks between the German states failed in 1848, and the confederation briefly dissolved but was re-established in 1850. |
| North German Confederation | The North German Confederation , came into existence in August 1866 as a military alliance of 22 states of northern Germany with the Kingdom of Prussia as the leading state. In July 1867 it was transformed into a federal state. It provided the country with a constitution and was the building block of the German Empire, which adopted most parts of the federation"s constitution and its flag. |
| Hohenzollern-Sigmaringen | The House of Hohenzollern-Sigmaringen is the cadet branch of the senior Swabian branch of the Hohenzollern dynasty, less known than the Franconian branch which became Burgraves of Nuremberg and later ruled Brandenburg-Prussia and the German Empire. The state which the cadet branch ruled was the County of Hohenzollern-Sigmaringen , which later became a principality (Fürstentum Hohenzollern-Sigmaringen). |

| | |
|---|---|
| | The County of Hohenzollern-Sigmaringen was created in 1576, upon the partition of the County of Hohenzollern, a fief of the Holy Roman Empire. |
| German Empire | The German Empire is the name commonly used in English to describe Germany from the unification of Germany and proclamation of Wilhelm I as German Emperor on 18 January 1871 to 1918, when it became a German republic after defeat in World War I and the abdication of Wilhelm II . The term Second Reich is sometimes applied to the period from 1871 to 1918 although, after the collapse of Hitler"s Third Reich, the term has generally fallen out of popularity. During its 47 years of existence, the German Empire emerged as one of the most powerful industrial economies in the world and a formidable great power, until it collapsed following its military defeat in World War I and the concurrent November Revolution. |
| Austria-Hungary | Austria-Hungary the Dual Monarchy or the k.u.k Monarchy, was a state in Central Europe ruled by the House of Habsburg, constitutionally a monarchic union between the crowns of the Austrian Empire and the Kingdom of Hungary. The state was a result of the Ausgleich or Compromise of 1867, under which the Austrian Habsburgs agreed to share power with a separate Hungarian government, dividing the territory of the former Austrian Empire between them. The Dual Monarchy existed for 51 years until 1918, when it dissolved following military defeat in the First World War. |
| Brandenburg-Prussia | Brandenburg-Prussia was a German monarchy established by the personal union between the Duchy of Prussia and the Margraviate of Brandenburg in 1618. The monarchy was ruled by the branch of the Hohenzollern dynasty that had earlier ruled Brandenburg. The term Brandenburg-Prussia refers to this monarchy from its establishment until 1701, after which it is usually known as the Kingdom of Prussia. |
| Oireachtas | From 1922 to 1937 the Oireachtas was the legislature of the Irish Free State. Until the final days of the Irish Free State it consisted of the King and two houses: Dáil Éireann and Seanad Éireann (also known as the "Senate"). Like the modern Oireachtas, the Free State legislature was dominated by the powerful, directly elected Dáil. |
| October | October Â·) is the tenth month of the year in the Gregorian Calendar and one of seven Gregorian months with a length of 31 days. The eighth month in the old Roman calendar, October retained its name when January and February were added. When the calendar was originally created by the Romans, the year began in March this meant that instead of October being the 10th month of the year it was originally the 8th month of the year. |
| Peasant | A Peasant is an agricultural worker who subsists by working a small plot of ground. The term Peasant today is sometimes used in a pejorative sense for impoverished farmers. Peasants typically make up the majority of the agricultural labour force in a Pre-industrial society, dependent on the cultivation of their land: without stockpiles of provisions they thrive or starve according to the most recent harvest. |

| | |
|---|---|
| Revolution | A Revolution is a fundamental change in power or organizational structures that takes place in a relatively short period of time. Aristotle described two types of political Revolution<br><br>· Complete change from one constitution to another<br>· Modification of an existing constitution.<br>Revolution s have occurred through human history and vary widely in terms of methods, duration, and motivating ideology. |
| Confederate States of America | The Confederate States of America formed as the government set up from 1861 to 1865 by eleven southern slave states of the United States of America, each of which had previously declared their secession from the United States. The CSA"s control over its claimed territory varied during the course of the American Civil War, depending on the success of its military.<br>Asserting that states had a right to secede, seven states declared their independence from the United States before the inauguration of Abraham Lincoln as President on March 4, 1861; four more did so after the Civil War began at the Battle of Fort Sumter. |
| Liberal Party | Liberal Party is the name of dozens of political parties around the world. It usually designates a party that is ideologically liberal, meaning that they advocate individual rights and civil liberties, and sometimes left wing, meaning that they are reliant on governmental solutions to social and economic problems. There are also some Liberal Parties which subscribe to classical liberalism and therefore support a mostly unregulated free market. |
| September | September Â·) is the ninth month of the year in the Gregorian Calendar and one of four Gregorian months with 30 days.<br>In Latin, septem means "seven" and septimus means "seventh"; September was in fact the seventh month of the Roman calendar until 153 BC, when the first month changed from Kalendas Martius to Kalendas Januarius (1 January). In the Northern hemisphere, the beginning of the meteorological autumn is 1 September. |
| Slavery | Slavery (Romanian: robie) existed on the territory of present-day Romania from before the founding of the principalities of Wallachia and Moldavia in 13th-14th century, until it was abolished in stages during the 1840s and 1850s. Most of the slaves were of Roma (Gypsy) ethnicity. Particularly in Moldavia there were also slaves of Tatar ethnicity, probably prisoners captured from the wars with the Nogai and Crimean Tatars. |
| Canada | CANADA is a country occupying most of northern North America, extending from the Atlantic Ocean in the east to the Pacific Ocean in the west and northward into the Arctic Ocean. It is the world"s second largest country by total area and shares the world"s longest common border with the United States to the south and northwest.<br>The land occupied by CANADA was inhabited for millennia by various groups of Aboriginal people. |

| | |
|---|---|
| Declaration of Independence | A Declaration of independence is an assertion of the independence of an aspiring state or states. Such places are usually declared from part or all of the territory of another nation or failed nation, or are breakaway territories from within the larger state. Not all declarations of independence were successful and resulted in independence for these regions. |
| Union of Soviet Socialist Republics | The Union of Soviet Socialist Republics (USSR) was a constitutionally socialist state that existed in Eurasia from 1922 to 1991. The name is a translation of the Russian: Â·), tr. Soyuz Sovetskikh Sotsialisticheskikh Respublik, abbreviated Ð¡Ð¡Ð¡Ð , SSSR. The common short name is Soviet Union, from Ð¡Ð¾Ð²ÐµÑ‚Ñ Ð°Ð¸Ð¹ Ð¡Ð¾ÑŽÐ··, Sovetskiy Soyuz. |
| Michael | Michael is a given name that comes from the Hebrew: žÖ´×™×›Ö¸× Öµ×œ / ×ž×™×›×™× ×œ×²×â€Ž , meaning "Who is like God?" In English, it is sometimes shortened to Mike, Mikey, or, especially in Ireland, Mick. Michael is one of the Archangels. Female forms of Michael include Michele, Michelle, Michaela, Mechelle, Micheline, and Michaelle, although there are women with the name Michael, such as Michael Learned. |
| Scientific method | Scientific method refers to a body of techniques for investigating phenomena, acquiring new knowledge, or correcting and integrating previous knowledge. To be termed scientific, a method of inquiry must be based on gathering observable, empirical and measurable evidence subject to specific principles of reasoning. A Scientific method consists of the collection of data through observation and experimentation, and the formulation and testing of hypotheses. |
| Holy Roman Empire | The Holy Roman Empire ) was a union of territories in Central Europe during the Middle Ages and the Early Modern period under a Holy Roman Emperor. The first emperor of the Holy Roman Empire was Otto I, crowned in 962. The last was Francis II, who abdicated and dissolved the Empire in 1806 during the Napoleonic Wars. |
| Nazi Germany | Nazi Germany and the Third Reich are the common English names for Germany between 1933 and 1945, while it was led by Adolf Hitler and the National Socialist German Worker"s Party . The name Third Reich (Drittes Reich, "Third Reich") refers to the state as the successor to the Holy Roman Empire of the Middle Ages and the German Empire of 1871-1918. In German, the state was known as Deutsches Reich until 1943, when its official name became Großdeutsches Reich . |
| Roman | A Roman or civil diocese was one of the administrative divisions of the later Roman Empire, starting with the Tetrarchy. It formed the intermediate level of government, grouping several provinces and being in turn subordinated to a praetorian prefecture. The earliest use of "diocese" as an administrative unit was in the Greek-speaking East. |
| August | August Â·) is the eighth month of the year in the Gregorian Calendar and one of seven Gregorian months with a length of 31 days. |

This month was originally named Sextilis in Latin, because it was the sixth month in the original ten-month Roman calendar under Romulus in 753 BC, when March was the first month of the year. About 700 BC it became the eighth month when January and February were added to the year before March by King Numa Pompilius, who also gave it 29 days.

| | |
|---|---|
| Alexander | Alexander was tagus or despot of Pherae in Thessaly, and ruled from 369 BC to 358 BC. The accounts of his usurpation vary somewhat in minor points. Diodorus Siculus tells us that on the assassination of his father, the tyrant Jason of Pherae, in 370 BC, his brother Polydorus ruled for a year, and was then poisoned by Alexander, another brother. According to Xenophon, Polydorus was murdered by his brother Polyphron, and Polyphron, in 369 BC murdered by Alexander--his nephew, according to Plutarch, who relates also that Alexander worshiped the spear with which he slew his uncle as if it was a god. |
| Industrial Revolution | The Industrial Revolution was a period in the late 18th and early 19th centuries where major changes in agriculture, manufacturing, mining, and transport had a profound effect on the socioeconomic and cultural conditions in the United Kingdom. The changes subsequently spread throughout Europe, North America, and eventually the world. The onset of the Industrial Revolution marked a major turning point in human society; almost every aspect of daily life was eventually influenced in some way. |
| Party | A Party is a gathering of people who have been invited by a host for the purposes of socializing, conversation, and recreation. A Party will typically feature food and beverages, and often music and dancing as well. Some parties are held in honor of a specific person, day, or event (e.g., a birthday Party, a Super Bowl Party, or a St. Patrick"s Day Party). |
| Second Industrial Revolution | The Second Industrial Revolution was a phase of the Industrial Revolution; sometimes labeled as the separate Technical Revolution. From a technological and a social point of view there is no clean break between the two. Major innovations during the period occurred in the chemical, electrical, petroleum, and steel industries. |
| Social Democratic Party | The Social Democratic Party (Romanian: Partidul Social Democrat, PSD) is a major political party of Romania. It can be loosely classified as a center-left party, although the right-left division in Romania is quite blurred. After the 2008 Romanian legislative elections the party entered in coalition with the Democratic Liberal Party (PD-L) and formed a government led by Emil Boc, the president of the PD-L. Previously, from 2005 to 2008, the PSD was an opposition party, after it lost the 2004 legislative election to the now-defunct Justice and Truth Alliance, comprising the National Liberal Party and Democratic Party. |
| Declaration of Independence | A Declaration of independence is an assertion of the independence of an aspiring state or states. Such places are usually declared from part or all of the territory of another nation or failed nation, or are breakaway territories from within the larger state. Not all declarations of independence were successful and resulted in independence for these regions. |
| France | France or ; French: [fɛ́ɛ́ìʃs]), officially the French Republic , is a country located in Western Europe, with several overseas islands and territories located on other continents. Metropolitan France extends from the Mediterranean Sea to the English Channel and the North Sea, and from the Rhine to the Atlantic Ocean. It is often referred to as L"Hexagone ("The Hexagon") because of the geometric shape of its territory. |

| | |
|---|---|
| Green Party | A Green Party or ecologist party is a formally organized political party based on the principles of Green politics. These principles include environmentalism, reliance on grassroots democracy, nonviolence, and support for social justice causes, including those related to the rights of indigenous peoples, among others. "Greens" believe that the exercise of these principles leads to the health of people, societies, and ecosystems. |
| Japan | Japan participated in World War I from 1914 to 1917, as one of the major Entente Powers and played an important role in securing the sea lanes in South Pacific and Indian Oceans against the Kaiserliche Marine. Politically, Japan seized the opportunity to expand its sphere of influence in China, and to gain recognition as a great power in postwar geopolitics.<br>On 7 August 1914, the Japanese government received an official request from the British government for assistance in destroying the German raiders of the Kaiserliche Marine in and around Chinese waters. |
| Factory | A Factory (previously manuFactory) or manufacturing plant is an industrial building where workers manufacture goods or supervise machines processing one product into another. Most modern factories have large warehouses or warehouse-like facilities that contain heavy equipment used for assembly line production. Typically, factories gather and concentrate resources: workers, capital and plant. |
| August | August Â·) is the eighth month of the year in the Gregorian Calendar and one of seven Gregorian months with a length of 31 days.<br>This month was originally named Sextilis in Latin, because it was the sixth month in the original ten-month Roman calendar under Romulus in 753 BC, when March was the first month of the year. About 700 BC it became the eighth month when January and February were added to the year before March by King Numa Pompilius, who also gave it 29 days. |
| Law | The great end, for which men entered into society, was to secure their property. That right is preserved sacred and incommunicable in all instances, where it has not been taken away or abridged by some public Law for the good of the whole ... If no excuse can be found or produced, the silence of the books is an authority against the defendant, and the plaintiff must have judgment. |
| Force | In physics, a Force is any external agent that causes a change in the motion of a free body, or that causes stress in a fixed body. It can also be described by intuitive concepts such as a push or pull that can cause an object with mass to change its velocity , i.e., to accelerate, or which can cause a flexible object to deform. Force has both magnitude and direction, making it a vector quantity. |
| Parti | A Parti or Parti pris / from the French Prendre Parti meaning " to make a decision " , often referred to as the big idea , is the chief organizing thought or decision behind an Architect"s design presented in the form of a basic diagram and / or a simple statement. . |

| | |
|---|---|
| Austria-Hungary | Austria-Hungary the Dual Monarchy or the k.u.k Monarchy, was a state in Central Europe ruled by the House of Habsburg, constitutionally a monarchic union between the crowns of the Austrian Empire and the Kingdom of Hungary. The state was a result of the Ausgleich or Compromise of 1867, under which the Austrian Habsburgs agreed to share power with a separate Hungarian government, dividing the territory of the former Austrian Empire between them. The Dual Monarchy existed for 51 years until 1918, when it dissolved following military defeat in the First World War. |
| Day | A Day (symbol d) is a unit of time equivalent to approximately 24 hours. It is not an SI unit but it is accepted for use with SI. The SI unit of time is the second.<br>The word "Day" can also refer to the (roughly) half of the Day that is not night, also known as "Daytime". |
| Democratic Labor Party | The Democratic Labor Party is a political party in Australia that espouses social conservatism and opposes neo-liberalism. It is descended from, but not legally the same as, the Democratic Labor Party which existed from 1955 to 1978, and which until 1974 played an important role in Australian politics. At the 2006 Victorian election, the new Democratic Labor Party won parliamentary representation for the first time when it won a seat in the Victorian Legislative Council. |
| May | May Â·) is the fifth month of the year in the Gregorian Calendar and one of seven Gregorian months with the length of 31 days. It is also a month within the northern season of spring.<br>The month May has been named for the Greek goddess Maia, who was identified with the Roman era goddess of fertility, Bona Dea, whose festival was held in May. |
| Koinon | The Koinon (or "League") of Free Laconians was established in 21 BC by the Emperor Augustus, giving formal structure to a group of cities that had been associated for almost two centuries.<br>The Eleutherolakones (á¼ˉλευθερολÎˉκωνες, free Laconians) are first mentioned in 195 BC, after Sparta"s defeat in the Roman-Spartan War. The Roman general Titus Quinctius Flaminius placed several coastal cities of the Mani Peninsula under the protection of the Achean League, freeing them from Spartan hegemony. |
| Michael | Michael is a given name that comes from the Hebrew: žÖ´×™×›Ö¸× Öµ×œ / ×ž×™×›×›× ×œ×€Ž , meaning "Who is like God?" In English, it is sometimes shortened to Mike, Mikey, or, especially in Ireland, Mick.<br>Michael is one of the Archangels.<br>Female forms of Michael include Michele, Michelle, Michaela, Mechelle, Micheline, and Michaelle, although there are women with the name Michael, such as Michael Learned. |

**Congress**

The 2001 Congress of the Greens/Green Party USA, held at Carbondale, Illinois, was a critical event in the history of the Green Party in the United States. At the Congress, occurring July 20 to July 23, at which the G/GPUSA was to consider the Boston Proposal , a tentative "merger" agreement between it and the Association of State Green Parties (ASGP). After an intense internal organizational struggle, most of which revolved around whether or not to "accredit" various delegations (and thus grant the individuals within them voting privileges), the proposal was rejected; although 55% of the members in attendance voted to approve it (99 in favor, 81 against), the organization"s bylaws required yes votes from a "super-majority" of 66.7% of the delegates in attendance to pass.

**Greece**

Greece entered World War II on 28 October 1940, when the Italian army invaded from Albania. The Greek army dealt the first victory for the Allies by defeating the invasion and pushing Mussolini"s forces back into Albania. Hitler was reluctantly forced to send his own forces to overcome Greece in April 1941, and delay the invasion of the Soviet Union by six weeks.

**Ottoman**

The state of the Ottomans which began as part of the Anatolian Seljuk Sultanate and became an independent Empire, has been known historically by different names at different periods and in various languages. This page surveys the history of these names and their usage.

· Modern Turkish: OsmanlÄ± BeyliÄŸi;
The first declaration of statehood happened under Osman I.

· Ä€l-e Uá¹mÄ n

· Medieval Latin: Turchia
· Medieval Latin: Imperium Turcicum
· English: Turkey ; the current use of the name Turkey refers to the Republic of Turkey which succeeded the Ottoman Empire in 1923
· English: Turkish Empire, Ottoman Empire, Osmanic Empire, Osmanian Empire
· Ottoman Turkish/Persian: Ø¯ÙˆÙ„ Øª Ø¹Ù„ÙŠÙ‡ Ø¹Ø«Ù……Ø§Ù†ÙŠÙ‡ Devlet-i Âliye-yi Osmâniyye
· Ottoman Turkish/Persian: Devlet-i Âliye (The Sublime State)
· Ottoman Turkish/Persian: Devlet-i Ebed-Müddet
· Ottoman Turkish/Persian: Memâlik-i Mahrûse (The Well-Protected Domains)
· Ottoman Turkish/Persian: Memâlik-i Mahrûse-i Osmanî
· Modern Turkish: OsmanlÄ± Ä°mparatorluÄŸu (Ottoman Empire),
· Arabic: Ø§Ù„Ø¯ÙˆÙ„Ø©Ù Ø§Ù„Ø¹Ù„ÙŠØ©Ù Ø§Ù„Ø¹Ø«Ù……Ø§Ù†ÙŠØ©Ù  Ad-Dawlat al-Ê¤Ä€lÄ« al-Ê¤UthmÄ nÄ««
· Bulgarian: ÐžÑ Ð¼Ð°Ð½Ñ ÐºÐ° Ð¸Ð¼Ð¿ÐµÑ€Ð¸Ñ  (Osmanska Imperia)
· Greek: ÎŸÎ¸Ï‰Î¼Î±Î½Î¹ÎºÎ® Î'Ï…Ï„Î¿ÎºÏ€Î±Ï„Î¿Ï Î± (Osmanyan Kaysroutyoun)
· Armenian: Õ•Õ½Õ´Õ¡Õ¶Õ¥Õ¡Õ¶ Ô¿Õ¡ÕµÕ½Ö€Õ¸Ö‚Õ©ÕµÕ¸Ö‚Õ¶ (Osmanyan Kaysroutyoun)
In diplomatic circles, the Ottoman government was often referred to as the "Sublime Porte", a literal translation of the Ottoman Turkish Bâb-Ä± Âlî, which was the only gate of the imperial TopkapÄ± Palace that was open to foreigners, and where the Sultan, Grand Vizier or Viziers greeted the ambassadors.

| | |
|---|---|
| Popular Front | A Popular Front is a broad coalition of different political groupings, often made up of leftists and centrists who are united by opposition to another group (most often capitalist groups). Being very broad, they can sometimes include centrist and liberal (or "bourgeois") forces as well as socialist and communist ("working-class") groups. Popular Fronts are larger in scope than united fronts, which contain only working-class groups. |
| Portugal | Portugal , officially the Portuguese Republic (Portuguese: República Portuguesa), is a country on the Iberian Peninsula, member of the European Union and one of the founding members of NATO. Located in southwestern Europe, Portugal is the westernmost country of mainland Europe and is bordered by the Atlantic Ocean to the west and south and by Spain to the north and east. The Atlantic archipelagos of the Azores and Madeira are also part of Portugal. <br><br> The land within the borders of today"s Portuguese Republic has been continuously settled since prehistoric times. |
| Rebellion | Rebellion is a refusal of obedience. It may, therefore, be seen as encompassing a range of behaviors from civil disobedience and mass nonviolent resistance, to violent and organized attempts to destroy an established authority such as the government. Those who participate in Rebellions are known as "rebels". |
| Serbia | Serbia (Serbian: Đ¡Ñ€Đ±Đ¸Ñ˜Đ°, Srbija), officially the Republic of Serbia (Serbian: Đ Đµ¿ÑƒĐ±Đ»Đ¸Đ°°Đ Đ¡Ñ€Đ±Đ¸Ñ˜Đ°, Republika Srbija), is a country located in both Central and Southeastern Europe. Its territory covers the southern part of the Pannonian Plain and central part of the Balkans. Serbia borders Hungary to the north; Romania and Bulgaria to the east; the Republic of Macedonia to the south; and Croatia, Bosnia and Herzegovina and Montenegro to the west. |
| Revolution | A Revolution is a fundamental change in power or organizational structures that takes place in a relatively short period of time. Aristotle described two types of political Revolution <br><br> · Complete change from one constitution to another <br> · Modification of an existing constitution. <br> Revolution s have occurred through human history and vary widely in terms of methods, duration, and motivating ideology. |
| Howard | Howard is a popular English language occupational given name of Old English origin, meaning "noble watchman". Its nickname is "Howie" and its shortened form is "Ward" . Between 1900-1960, Howard ranked in the U.S. Top 200; between 1960-1990, it ranked in the U.S. Top 400; between 1990-2004, it ranked in the U.S. Top 600. |
| Peasant | A Peasant is an agricultural worker who subsists by working a small plot of ground. The term Peasant today is sometimes used in a pejorative sense for impoverished farmers. <br><br> Peasants typically make up the majority of the agricultural labour force in a Pre-industrial society, dependent on the cultivation of their land: without stockpiles of provisions they thrive or starve according to the most recent harvest. |

| | |
|---|---|
| Central Powers | The Central Powers was one of the two sides that participated in World War I, the other being the Entente Powers.<br>The Central Powers consisted of the German Empire, the Austrian-Hungarian Empire, the Ottoman Empire and the Kingdom of Bulgaria. The name "Central Powers" is derived from the location of these countries. |
| Hall | In architecture, several things are commonly known as Halls or Halls. A Hall is fundamentally a relatively large space enclosed by a roof and walls. In the Iron Age, a mead Hall was such a simple building and was the residence of a lord and his retainers. |
| Politics | Politics is a process by which groups of people make decisions. The term is generally applied to behavior within civil governments, but Politics has been observed in all human group interactions, including corporate, academic and religious institutions. It consists of "social relations involving authority or power" and refers to the regulation of a political unit, and to the methods and tactics used to formulate and apply policy. |
| Paris Commune | The Paris Commune was a government that briefly ruled Paris, from March 28 to May 28, 1871. It existed before the split between anarchists and socialists had taken place, and it is hailed by both groups as the first assumption of power by the working class. Debates over the policies and outcome of the Commune contributed to the break between those two political groups. |
| Republic | A Republic is a form of government in which the head of state is not a monarch and the people (or at least a part of its people) have an impact on its government. The word "Republic" is derived from the Latin phrase res publica which can be translated as "public affairs".<br>Both modern and ancient Republics vary widely in their ideology and composition. |
| National Assembly | Foreign relations<br>Democracy movement in Nepal<br>Civil War |
| | Other countries Â· Atlas<br>Politics portal |
| | The National Assembly (Nepali: Rashtriya Sabha) was the upper house of parliament in Nepal during the 1990 Constitution. It Nepal had 60 members, 10 nominated by the king, 35 elected by the House of Representatives and the remaining 15 elected by an electoral college made up of chairs of villages and towns. The legislature had a six-year term, and could be dissolved by the king. |
| Philippines | The Philippines (Tagalog: Pilipinas [pÉªlÉªË^pinÉ s]) officially known as the Republic of the Philippines, is a country in Southeast Asia with Manila as its capital city. It comprises 7,107 islands in the western Pacific Ocean.<br>The Philippines is the world"s 12th most populous country, with an estimated population of about 92 million people. |

Canada

CANADA is a country occupying most of northern North America, extending from the Atlantic Ocean in the east to the Pacific Ocean in the west and northward into the Arctic Ocean. It is the world"s second largest country by total area and shares the world"s longest common border with the United States to the south and northwest.

The land occupied by CANADA was inhabited for millennia by various groups of Aboriginal people.

Constitution

A Constitution is set of rules for government--often codified as a written document--that establishes principles of an autonomous political entity. In the case of countries, this term refers specifically to a national Constitution defining the fundamental political principles, and establishing the structure, procedures, powers and duties, of a government. By limiting the government"s own reach, most Constitutions guarantee certain rights to the people.

Austrian Empire

The Austrian Empire was a modern era successor empire founded on a remnant of the Holy Roman Empire centered on what is today"s Austria that officially lasted from 1804 to 1867. It was followed by combining the Royal House with that of Hungary creating the dual monarchy Austria-Hungary , which itself as one of the losers was dissolved at the end of World War I and broken into separate new states).

The term "Austrian Empire" is also used for the Habsburg possessions before 1804, which had no official collective name, although Austria is more frequent; the term of Austria-Hungary has also been used, incorrectly.

Tsar

Tsar or czar , Ukrainian: Ñ†Ð°Ñ€, in Serbian: Ñ†Ð°Ñ€ / car, in scientific transliteration respectively car" and car), occasionally spelled csar or tzar in English, is a Slavic term with Bulgarian origins used to designate certain monarchs. The first ruler to adopt the title Tsar was Simeon I of Bulgaria

Originally, the title Czar " href="/wiki/Caesar_(title)">Caesar) meant Emperor in the European medieval sense of the term, that is, a ruler who claims the same rank as a Roman emperor, with the approval of another emperor or a supreme ecclesiastical official (the Pope or the Ecumenical Patriarch).

Occasionally, the word could be used to designate other, non-Christian, supreme rulers.

| | |
|---|---|
| African Americans | Due to the prevailing social climate that existed in the United States after World War II, one in which racism was a prominent factor, African Americans did not benefit from the provisions of the G. I. Bill of Rights as much as their white counterparts. Though the bill did provide a more level playing field than the one blacks faced during Reconstruction, this is not saying much. Representative John Elliott Rankin, an economic liberal who was also an avid segregationalist and racist, sponsored the bill in the United States House of Representatives. |
| Mari | Mari (modern Tell Hariri, Syria) was an ancient Sumerian and Amorite city, located 11 kilometers north-west of the modern town of Abu Kamal on the western bank of Euphrates river, some 120 km southeast of Deir ez-Zor, Syria. It is thought to have been inhabited since the 5th millennium BC, although it flourished from 2900 BC until 1759 BC, when it was sacked by Hammurabi.<br><br>Mari was discovered in 1933 on the eastern flank of Syria, near the Iraqi border. |
| Industrial Revolution | The Industrial Revolution was a period in the late 18th and early 19th centuries where major changes in agriculture, manufacturing, mining, and transport had a profound effect on the socioeconomic and cultural conditions in the United Kingdom. The changes subsequently spread throughout Europe, North America, and eventually the world. The onset of the Industrial Revolution marked a major turning point in human society; almost every aspect of daily life was eventually influenced in some way. |
| Revolutionary | A Revolutionary is a person who either actively participates in, or advocates revolution. Also, when used as an adjective, the term Revolutionary refers to something that has a major, sudden impact on society or on some aspect of human endeavour. The term--both as a noun and adjective--is usually applied to the field of politics, and is occasionally used in the context of science, invention or art. |
| Scientific Revolution | In the history of science, the Scientific revolution was a period when new ideas in physics, astronomy, biology, human anatomy, chemistry, and other sciences led to a rejection of doctrines that had prevailed from Ancient Greece through the Middle Ages, and laid the foundation of modern science. According to the majority of scholars, the Scientific revolution began with the publication of two works that changed the course of science in 1543 and continued through the late 17th century: Nicolaus Copernicus"s De revolutionibus orbium coelestium (On the Revolutions of the Heavenly Spheres) and Andreas Vesalius"s De humani corporis fabrica (On the Fabric of the Human body.)<br><br>Philosopher and historian Alexandre Koyré coined the term Scientific revolution in 1939 to describe this epoch. |
| Austria-Hungary | Austria-Hungary the Dual Monarchy or the k.u.k Monarchy, was a state in Central Europe ruled by the House of Habsburg, constitutionally a monarchic union between the crowns of the Austrian Empire and the Kingdom of Hungary. The state was a result of the Ausgleich or Compromise of 1867, under which the Austrian Habsburgs agreed to share power with a separate Hungarian government, dividing the territory of the former Austrian Empire between them. The Dual Monarchy existed for 51 years until 1918, when it dissolved following military defeat in the First World War. |
| Austrian Empire | The Austrian Empire was a modern era successor empire founded on a remnant of the Holy Roman Empire centered on what is today"s Austria that officially lasted from 1804 to 1867. It was followed by combining the Royal House with that of Hungary creating the dual monarchy Austria-Hungary , which itself as one of the losers was dissolved at the end of World War I and broken into separate new states). |

The term "Austrian Empire" is also used for the Habsburg possessions before 1804, which had no official collective name, although Austria is more frequent; the term of Austria-Hungary has also been used, incorrectly.

| | |
|---|---|
| Houston Stewart Chamberlain | Houston Stewart Chamberlain (September 9, 1855 - January 9, 1927) was a British-born author of books on political philosophy, natural science and his posthumous father-in-law Richard Wagner. His two-volume book Die Grundlagen des Neunzehnten Jahrhunderts, whose title translates from the original German as The Foundations Of The Nineteenth Century and which was published in 1899, became one of the many references for the pan-Germanic movement of the early 20th century, and, later, of the antisemitism of Nazi racial philosophy.<br>Houston Stewart Chamberlain was born in Southsea, Hampshire, England. |
| Colonization | Colonization, , occurs whenever any one or more species populate an area. The term, which is derived from the Latin colere, "to inhabit, cultivate, frequent, practice, tend, guard, respect," originally related to humans. However, 19th century biogeographers dominated the term to describe the activities of birds, bacteria, or plant species. |
| Alexander | Alexander was tagus or despot of Pherae in Thessaly, and ruled from 369 BC to 358 BC.<br>The accounts of his usurpation vary somewhat in minor points. Diodorus Siculus tells us that on the assassination of his father, the tyrant Jason of Pherae, in 370 BC, his brother Polydorus ruled for a year, and was then poisoned by Alexander, another brother. According to Xenophon, Polydorus was murdered by his brother Polyphron, and Polyphron, in 369 BC murdered by Alexander--his nephew, according to Plutarch, who relates also that Alexander worshiped the spear with which he slew his uncle as if it was a god. |
| Nazi Germany | Nazi Germany and the Third Reich are the common English names for Germany between 1933 and 1945, while it was led by Adolf Hitler and the National Socialist German Worker"s Party . The name Third Reich (Drittes Reich, "Third Reich") refers to the state as the successor to the Holy Roman Empire of the Middle Ages and the German Empire of 1871-1918. In German, the state was known as Deutsches Reich until 1943, when its official name became Großdeutsches Reich . |
| Liberal Party | Liberal Party is the name of dozens of political parties around the world. It usually designates a party that is ideologically liberal, meaning that they advocate individual rights and civil liberties, and sometimes left wing, meaning that they are reliant on governmental solutions to social and economic problems. There are also some Liberal Parties which subscribe to classical liberalism and therefore support a mostly unregulated free market. |
| Force | In physics, a Force is any external agent that causes a change in the motion of a free body, or that causes stress in a fixed body. It can also be described by intuitive concepts such as a push or pull that can cause an object with mass to change its velocity , i.e., to accelerate, or which can cause a flexible object to deform. Force has both magnitude and direction, making it a vector quantity. |

| | |
|---|---|
| Canada | CANADA is a country occupying most of northern North America, extending from the Atlantic Ocean in the east to the Pacific Ocean in the west and northward into the Arctic Ocean. It is the world"s second largest country by total area and shares the world"s longest common border with the United States to the south and northwest.<br>The land occupied by CANADA was inhabited for millennia by various groups of Aboriginal people. |
| France | France or ; French: [fɛ ɛ'lʃs]), officially the French Republic , is a country located in Western Europe, with several overseas islands and territories located on other continents. Metropolitan France extends from the Mediterranean Sea to the English Channel and the North Sea, and from the Rhine to the Atlantic Ocean. It is often referred to as L"Hexagone ("The Hexagon") because of the geometric shape of its territory. |
| Rebellion | Rebellion is a refusal of obedience. It may, therefore, be seen as encompassing a range of behaviors from civil disobedience and mass nonviolent resistance, to violent and organized attempts to destroy an established authority such as the government. Those who participate in Rebellions are known as "rebels". |
| Republic | A Republic is a form of government in which the head of state is not a monarch and the people (or at least a part of its people) have an impact on its government. The word "Republic" is derived from the Latin phrase res publica which can be translated as "public affairs".<br>Both modern and ancient Republics vary widely in their ideology and composition. |
| Green Party | A Green Party or ecologist party is a formally organized political party based on the principles of Green politics. These principles include environmentalism, reliance on grassroots democracy, nonviolence, and support for social justice causes, including those related to the rights of indigenous peoples, among others. "Greens" believe that the exercise of these principles leads to the health of people, societies, and ecosystems. |
| Social Democratic Party | The Social Democratic Party (Romanian: Partidul Social Democrat, PSD) is a major political party of Romania. It can be loosely classified as a center-left party, although the right-left division in Romania is quite blurred. After the 2008 Romanian legislative elections the party entered in coalition with the Democratic Liberal Party (PD-L) and formed a government led by Emil Boc, the president of the PD-L. Previously, from 2005 to 2008, the PSD was an opposition party, after it lost the 2004 legislative election to the now-defunct Justice and Truth Alliance, comprising the National Liberal Party and Democratic Party. |
| Duma | A Duma is any of various representative assemblies in modern Russia and Russian history. The State Duma in the Russian Empire and Russian Federation corresponds to the lower house of the parliament. Simply it is a form of Russian governmental institution, that was formed after the last Czar, Nicholas II. It is also the term for a council to early Russian rulers , as well as for city councils in Imperial Russia ("Municipal Dumas"), and city and regional legislative bodies in the Russian Federation. |

| | |
|---|---|
| October | October Â·) is the tenth month of the year in the Gregorian Calendar and one of seven Gregorian months with a length of 31 days. The eighth month in the old Roman calendar, October retained its name when January and February were added. When the calendar was originally created by the Romans, the year began in March this meant that instead of October being the 10th month of the year it was originally the 8th month of the year. |
| Revolution | A Revolution is a fundamental change in power or organizational structures that takes place in a relatively short period of time. Aristotle described two types of political Revolution<br><br>· Complete change from one constitution to another<br>· Modification of an existing constitution.<br>Revolution s have occurred through human history and vary widely in terms of methods, duration, and motivating ideology. |
| Imperialism | The term Imperialism commonly refers to a political or geographical domain such as the Ottoman Empire, the French Empire the Russian Empire, the Chinese Empire etc., but the term can equally be applied to domains of knowledge, beliefs, values and expertise, such as the empires of Christianity or Islam . Imperialism is usually autocratic, and also sometimes monolithic in character.<br>Imperialism is found in the ancient histories of the Assyrian Empire, Chinese Empire, Roman Empire, Greece, the Persian Empire, and the Ottoman Empire , ancient Egypt, India, the Aztec empire, and a basic component to the conquests of Genghis Khan and other warlords. |
| New imperialism | New Imperialism refers to the colonial expansion adopted by Europe"s powers and, later, Japan and the United States, during the 19th and early 20th centuries; expansion approximately took place from the Franco-Prussian War to World War I . The period is distinguished by an unprecedented pursuit of what has been termed "empire for empire"s sake," aggressive competition for overseas territorial acquisitions and the emergence in some colonizing countries of doctrines of racial superiority which purported to explain the unfitness of backward peoples for self-government.<br>The term imperialism was used from the third quarter of the nineteenth century to describe various forms of political control by a greater power over less powerful territories or nationalities, although analytically the phenomena which it denotes may differ greatly from each other and from the "New" imperialism. |
| Angola | Angola, officially the Republic of Angola , is a country in south-central Africa bordered by Namibia on the south, Democratic Republic of the Congo on the north, and Zambia on the east; its west coast is on the Atlantic Ocean. The exclave province of Cabinda has a border with the Republic of the Congo and the Democratic Republic of the Congo. Angola was a Portuguese overseas territory from the 16th century to 1975. |
| French colonies | "French Colonies" is the name used by philatelists to refer to the postage stamps issued by France for use in the parts of the French colonial empire that did not have stamps of their own. These were in use from 1859 to 1906, and from 1943 to 1945. French Colonies stamp 1859<br>The first of these were small square stamps issued in 1859, depicting an eagle and crown in a round frame, with the inscription "COLONIES DE L"EMPIRE FRANCAIS". |

| | |
|---|---|
| Orange Free State | The Republic of the Orange Free State (Afrikaans: Oranje-Vrystaat; Dutch: Oranje-Vrijstaat) was an independent Boer republic in southern Africa during the second half of the 19th century, and later a British colony and a province of the Union of South Africa. It is the historical precursor to the present-day Free State province. Extending between the Orange and Vaal rivers, its borders were determined by the United Kingdom in 1848 when the region was proclaimed as the Orange River Sovereignty, with a seat of a British Resident in Bloemfontein. |
| Portugal | Portugal , officially the Portuguese Republic (Portuguese: República Portuguesa), is a country on the Iberian Peninsula, member of the European Union and one of the founding members of NATO. Located in southwestern Europe, Portugal is the westernmost country of mainland Europe and is bordered by the Atlantic Ocean to the west and south and by Spain to the north and east. The Atlantic archipelagos of the Azores and Madeira are also part of Portugal.<br>The land within the borders of today"s Portuguese Republic has been continuously settled since prehistoric times. |
| Transvaal | The Transvaal (Afrikaans, lit. beyond the Vaal River) is the name of an area of northern South Africa. Originally the bulk of the independent Boer South African Republic, after the Anglo-Boer War of 1899-1902 it became the Transvaal Colony, and one of the founding provinces of the Union of South Africa, with its regional capital in Pretoria, from 1910 until 1994. The province no longer exists, and its territory now forms the provinces of Gauteng, Limpopo and Mpumalanga and part of the North West Province. |
| Tripoli | Tripoli is a city in Lebanon. Situated north of Batroun and the cape of Lithoprosopon, Tripoli is the capital of the North Governorate and the Tripoli District . The city is located 85 km north of the capital Beirut, and can be described as the easternmost port of Lebanon. |
| Australia | Australia , officially the Commonwealth of Australia, is a country in the Southern Hemisphere comprising the continental mainland (the world"s smallest), the island of Tasmania, and numerous smaller islands in the Indian and Pacific Oceans.[N4] Neighbouring countries include Indonesia, East Timor, and Papua New Guinea to the north, the Solomon Islands, Vanuatu, and New Caledonia to the north-east, and New Zealand to the southeast.<br>For some 40,000 years before European settlement commenced in the late 18th century, the Australian mainland and Tasmania were inhabited by around 250 individual nations of indigenous Australians. After sporadic visits by fishermen from the immediate north, and European discovery by Dutch explorers in 1606, the eastern half of Australia was claimed by the British in 1770 and initially settled through penal transportation to the colony of New South Wales, founded on 26 January 1788. |
| Imperialism in Asia | Imperialism in Asia traces its roots back to the late fifteenth century with a series of voyages that sought a sea passage to India in the hope of establishing direct trade between Europe and Asia in spices. Before 1500 European economies were largely self-sufficient, only supplemented by minor trade with Asia and Africa. Within the next century, however, European and Asian economies were slowly becoming integrated through the rise of new global trade routes; and the early thrust of European political power, commerce, and culture in Asia gave rise to a growing trade in lucrative commodities--a key development in the rise of today"s modern world free market economy. |

In the sixteenth century, the Portuguese established a monopoly over trade between Asia and Europe by managing to prevent rival powers from using the water routes between Europe and the Indian Ocean.

**East India Company**

The East India Company was an early English joint-stock company that was formed initially for pursuing trade with the East Indies, but that ended up trading mainly with the Indian subcontinent and China. The oldest among several similarly formed European East India Companies, the Company was granted an English Royal Charter, under the name Governor and Company of Merchants of London Trading into the East Indies, by Elizabeth I on 31 December 1600. After a rival English company challenged its monopoly in the late 17th century, the two companies were merged in 1708 to form the United Company of Merchants of England Trading to the East Indies, commonly styled the Honourable East India Company, and abbreviated, HEast India Company; the Company was colloquially referred to as John Company, and in India as Company Bahadur .

**India**

India, officially the Indian Empire, declared war on Germany in September 1939. The Provinces of India " href="/wiki/East_African_Campaign_(World_War_II)">East African Campaign, Western Desert Campaign and the Italian Campaign. At the height of the World War, more than 2.5 million Indian troops were fighting Axis forces around the globe.

**Ming dynasty**

During the Ming dynasty in China attempts were made to subjugate, control, tax, and settle ethnic Chinese along the lightly populated frontier of Yunnan with Southeast Asia . This frontier region was inhabited by many small Tai chieftainships or states as well as other Tibeto-Burman and Mon-Khmer ethnic groups.
The Ming Shi-lu records the relations between the Ming court in Beijing and the Tai-Yunnan frontier as well as Ming military actions and diplomacy along the frontier.

**Open door policy**

The Open Door Policy is a concept in foreign affairs. As a theory, the Open Door Policy originates with British commercial practice, as was reflected in treaties concluded with Qing Dynasty China after the First Opium War (1839-1842). Although the Open Door is generally associated with China, it was recognized at the Berlin Conference of 1885, which declared that no power could levy preferential duties in the Congo basin.

**Colony**

In politics and in history, a Colony is a territory under the immediate political control of a state. For colonies in antiquity, city-states would often found their own colonies. Some colonies were historically countries, while others were territories without definite statehood from their inception.

**Japan**

Japan participated in World War I from 1914 to 1917, as one of the major Entente Powers and played an important role in securing the sea lanes in South Pacific and Indian Oceans against the Kaiserliche Marine. Politically, Japan seized the opportunity to expand its sphere of influence in China, and to gain recognition as a great power in postwar geopolitics.
On 7 August 1914, the Japanese government received an official request from the British government for assistance in destroying the German raiders of the Kaiserliche Marine in and around Chinese waters.

| | |
|---|---|
| Burma Road | The Burma Road is a road linking Burma with China. Its terminals are Kunming, Yunnan and Lashio, Burma. When it was built, Burma was a British colony. |
| Philippines | The Philippines (Tagalog: Pilipinas [pɛˈlɪpaˈɛˆpinɛ s]) officially known as the Republic of the Philippines, is a country in Southeast Asia with Manila as its capital city. It comprises 7,107 islands in the western Pacific Ocean. The Philippines is the world"s 12th most populous country, with an estimated population of about 92 million people. |
| Puerto Rico | Puerto Rico , officially the Commonwealth of Puerto Rico , is an unincorporated territory of the United States located in the northeastern Caribbean, east of the Dominican Republic and west of the Virgin Islands. Puerto Rico, geographically, is composed of an archipelago that includes the main island of Puerto Rico and a number of smaller islands, the largest of which are Vieques, Culebra, and Mona. The main island of Puerto Rico is the smallest by land area and second smallest by population among the four Greater Antilles, which also include Cuba, Hispaniola, and Jamaica. Ethnically, the people of Puerto Rico, according to a Special Committee of the United Nations, "constitute a Latin American and Caribbean nation that has its own unequivocal national identity". |
| Tonkin | Tonkin (Báᵒ¯c Ká»³ in Vietnamese), also spelled Tongkin, Tonquin or Tongking, is the northernmost part of Vietnam, south of China"s Yunnan and Guangxi Provinces, east of northern Laos, and west of the Gulf of Tonkin. Locally, it is known as Báᵒ¯c Ká»³, meaning "Northern Region". Located on the fertile delta of the Red River, Tonkin is rich in rice production. |
| Boxer Rebellion | The Boxer Rebellion, more properly called the Boxer Uprising was a violent anti-imperialism, anti-Christian movement by the "Righteous Fists of Harmony," Yihe tuanä¹‰å'Œå›¢ or Society of Righteous and Harmonious Fists in China , between 1898 and 1901. In response to imperialist expansion, growth of cosmopolitan influences, and missionary evangelism, and against the backdrop of state fiscal crisis and natural disasters, local organizations began to emerge in Shandong in 1898. At first, they were relentlessly suppressed by the Manchu-led Qing Dynasty of China. |
| Congress | The 2001 Congress of the Greens/Green Party USA, held at Carbondale, Illinois, was a critical event in the history of the Green Party in the United States. At the Congress, occurring July 20 to July 23, at which the G/GPUSA was to consider the Boston Proposal , a tentative "merger" agreement between it and the Association of State Green Parties (ASGP). After an intense internal organizational struggle, most of which revolved around whether or not to "accredit" various delegations (and thus grant the individuals within them voting privileges), the proposal was rejected; although 55% of the members in attendance voted to approve it (99 in favor, 81 against), the organization"s bylaws required yes votes from a "super-majority" of 66.7% of the delegates in attendance to pass. |
| Indian National Congress | From its foundation on 28 December 1885 till the time of independence of India on August 15, 1947, the Indian National Congress was the largest and most prominent Indian public organization, and central and defining influence of the Indian Independence Movement. |

Although initially and primarily a political body, the Congress transformed itself into a national vehicle for social reform and human upliftment. And the Congress"s foundations in democracy and multiculturalism helped make India a consistently democratic and free nation.

**Koinon**

The Koinon (or "League") of Free Laconians was established in 21 BC by the Emperor Augustus, giving formal structure to a group of cities that had been associated for almost two centuries.

The Eleutherolakones (á¼˜λευθερολÎ¬κωνες, free Laconians) are first mentioned in 195 BC, after Sparta"s defeat in the Roman-Spartan War. The Roman general Titus Quinctius Flaminius placed several coastal cities of the Mani Peninsula under the protection of the Achean League, freeing them from Spartan hegemony.

**Montenegro**

Montenegro ( or /ËŒmÉ'ntÉˈËˆniË  É¡roËŠ/), ) (meaning "Black Mountain" in Montenegrin) is a country located in Southeastern Europe. It has a coast on the Adriatic Sea to the south-west and is bordered by Croatia to the west, Bosnia and Herzegovina to the northwest, Serbia to the northeast, Kosovo to the east and Albania to the south . Its capital and largest city is Podgorica, while Cetinje is designated as the Prijestonica (ÐŸÑ€Ð¸ÑˆÐµÑ Ñ‚Ð¾Ð½Ð¸Ñ†Ð°), meaning the former Royal Capital City..

**Ottoman**

The state of the Ottomans which began as part of the Anatolian Seljuk Sultanate and became an independent Empire, has been known historically by different names at different periods and in various languages. This page surveys the history of these names and their usage.

· Modern Turkish: OsmanlÄ± BeyliÄŸi;
The first declaration of statehood happened under Osman I.

· Ä€l-e Uá'mÄ  n

· Medieval Latin: Turchia
· Medieval Latin: Imperium Turcicum
· English: Turkey ; the current use of the name Turkey refers to the Republic of Turkey which succeeded the Ottoman Empire in 1923
· English: Turkish Empire, Ottoman Empire, Osmanic Empire, Osmanian Empire
· Ottoman Turkish/Persian: Ø¯ÙˆÙ„Øª Ø¹Ù„ÛŒÚ‡ Ø¹Ø«Ù…Ø§Ù†ÛŒÚ‡ Devlet-i Âliye-yi Osmâniyye
· Ottoman Turkish/Persian: Devlet-i Âliye (The Sublime State)
· Ottoman Turkish/Persian: Devlet-i Ebed-Müddet
· Ottoman Turkish/Persian: Memâlik-i Mahrûse (The Well-Protected Domains)
· Ottoman Turkish/Persian: Memâlik-i Mahrûse-i Osmanî
· Modern Turkish: OsmanlÄ± Ä°mparatorluÄŸu (Ottoman Empire),
· Arabic: Ø§Ù„Ø¯ÙˆÙ„Ø©Ù  Ø§Ù„Ø¹Ù„ÙŠØ©Ù  Ø§Ù„Ø¹Ø«Ù…Ø§Ù†ÙŠØ©Ù Ad-Dawlat al-ˈÄ€lÄ« al-ˈUthmÄ  nÄ«
· Bulgarian: ÐžÑ Ð¼Ð°Ð½Ñ ÐºÐ° Ð˜Ð¼Ð¿ÐµÑ€Ð¸Ñ  (Osmanska Imperia)
· Greek: ÎŸÎ¸Ï‰Î¼Î±Î½Î¹ÎºÎ® Î‘Ï…Ï„Î¿ÎºÏ€Î±Ï„Î¿Ï Î¯Î± 
· Armenian: Ô•Õ½Õ´Õ¡Õ¶Õ¥Õ¡Õ¶ Ô¿Õ¡Õ µÕ½Õ¥Ö€Õ¸Ö‚Õ©Õ µÕ¸Ö‚Õ¶ (Osmanyan Kaysroutyoun)

In diplomatic circles, the Ottoman government was often referred to as the "Sublime Porte", a literal translation of the Ottoman Turkish Bâb-Ä± Âlî, which was the only gate of the imperial TopkapÄ± Palace that was open to foreigners, and where the Sultan, Grand Vizier or Viziers greeted the ambassadors.

| | |
|---|---|
| Ottoman Empire | The Ottoman Empire or Ottoman State , also known by its contemporaries as the Turkish Empire or Turkey , was an empire that lasted from 1299 to November 1, 1922 (as an imperial monarchy) or July 24, 1923 (de jure, as a state.) It was succeeded by the Republic of Turkey, which was officially proclaimed on October 29, 1923. At the height of its power (16th-17th century), it spanned three continents, controlling much of Southeastern Europe, Western Asia and North Africa. |
| Serbia | Serbia (Serbian: Đ¡Ñ€Đ±Đ¸Ñ˜Đ°, Srbija), officially the Republic of Serbia (Serbian: Đ Đµอ¿Ñƒอ±อ»อ¸อºอ° Đ¡Ñ€Đ±Đ¸Ñ˜Đ°, Republika Srbija), is a country located in both Central and Southeastern Europe. Its territory covers the southern part of the Pannonian Plain and central part of the Balkans. Serbia borders Hungary to the north; Romania and Bulgaria to the east; the Republic of Macedonia to the south; and Croatia, Bosnia and Herzegovina and Montenegro to the west. |
| Balkan War | The Balkan Wars were two wars in South-eastern Europe in 1912-1913. The First Balkan War broke out on 8 October 1912 when Bulgaria, Greece, Montenegro and Serbia , having large parts of their ethnic populations under Ottoman sovereignty, attacked the Ottoman Empire, terminating its five-century rule in the Balkans in a seven-month campaign resulting in the Treaty of London. The Second Balkan War broke out on 16 June 1913 when Bulgaria, dissatisfied with its gains, attacked its former allies, Serbia and Greece. |
| Greece | Greece entered World War II on 28 October 1940, when the Italian army invaded from Albania. The Greek army dealt the first victory for the Allies by defeating the invasion and pushing Mussolini"s forces back into Albania. Hitler was reluctantly forced to send his own forces to overcome Greece in April 1941, and delay the invasion of the Soviet Union by six weeks. |

| | |
|---|---|
| Austria-Hungary | Austria-Hungary the Dual Monarchy or the k.u.k Monarchy, was a state in Central Europe ruled by the House of Habsburg, constitutionally a monarchic union between the crowns of the Austrian Empire and the Kingdom of Hungary. The state was a result of the Ausgleich or Compromise of 1867, under which the Austrian Habsburgs agreed to share power with a separate Hungarian government, dividing the territory of the former Austrian Empire between them. The Dual Monarchy existed for 51 years until 1918, when it dissolved following military defeat in the First World War. |
| Republic | A Republic is a form of government in which the head of state is not a monarch and the people (or at least a part of its people) have an impact on its government. The word "Republic" is derived from the Latin phrase res publica which can be translated as "public affairs". <br> Both modern and ancient Republics vary widely in their ideology and composition. |
| Brandenburg-Prussia | Brandenburg-Prussia was a German monarchy established by the personal union between the Duchy of Prussia and the Margraviate of Brandenburg in 1618. <br> The monarchy was ruled by the branch of the Hohenzollern dynasty that had earlier ruled Brandenburg. The term Brandenburg-Prussia refers to this monarchy from its establishment until 1701, after which it is usually known as the Kingdom of Prussia. |
| Alexander | Alexander was tagus or despot of Pherae in Thessaly, and ruled from 369 BC to 358 BC. <br> The accounts of his usurpation vary somewhat in minor points. Diodorus Siculus tells us that on the assassination of his father, the tyrant Jason of Pherae, in 370 BC, his brother Polydorus ruled for a year, and was then poisoned by Alexander, another brother. According to Xenophon, Polydorus was murdered by his brother Polyphron, and Polyphron, in 369 BC murdered by Alexander--his nephew, according to Plutarch, who relates also that Alexander worshiped the spear with which he slew his uncle as if it was a god. |
| Central Powers | The Central Powers was one of the two sides that participated in World War I, the other being the Entente Powers. <br> The Central Powers consisted of the German Empire, the Austrian-Hungarian Empire, the Ottoman Empire and the Kingdom of Bulgaria. The name "Central Powers" is derived from the location of these countries. |
| Lawrence | Lawrence is a city in Essex County, Massachusetts, United States on the Merrimack River. As of the 2000 census, the city had a total population of 72,043. Surrounding communities include Methuen to the north, Andover to the southwest, and North Andover to the southeast. |
| Australia | Australia , officially the Commonwealth of Australia, is a country in the Southern Hemisphere comprising the continental mainland (the world"s smallest), the island of Tasmania, and numerous smaller islands in the Indian and Pacific Oceans.[N4] Neighbouring countries include Indonesia, East Timor, and Papua New Guinea to the north, the Solomon Islands, Vanuatu, and New Caledonia to the north-east, and New Zealand to the southeast. |

For some 40,000 years before European settlement commenced in the late 18th century, the Australian mainland and Tasmania were inhabited by around 250 individual nations of indigenous Australians. After sporadic visits by fishermen from the immediate north, and European discovery by Dutch explorers in 1606, the eastern half of Australia was claimed by the British in 1770 and initially settled through penal transportation to the colony of New South Wales, founded on 26 January 1788.

**Industrial Revolution**

The Industrial Revolution was a period in the late 18th and early 19th centuries where major changes in agriculture, manufacturing, mining, and transport had a profound effect on the socioeconomic and cultural conditions in the United Kingdom. The changes subsequently spread throughout Europe, North America, and eventually the world. The onset of the Industrial Revolution marked a major turning point in human society; almost every aspect of daily life was eventually influenced in some way.

**Rebellion**

Rebellion is a refusal of obedience. It may, therefore, be seen as encompassing a range of behaviors from civil disobedience and mass nonviolent resistance, to violent and organized attempts to destroy an established authority such as the government. Those who participate in Rebellions are known as "rebels".

**Force**

In physics, a Force is any external agent that causes a change in the motion of a free body, or that causes stress in a fixed body. It can also be described by intuitive concepts such as a push or pull that can cause an object with mass to change its velocity , i.e., to accelerate, or which can cause a flexible object to deform. Force has both magnitude and direction, making it a vector quantity.

**March**

March Â·) is the third month of the year in the Gregorian Calendar, and one of the seven months which are 31 days long.
March in the Southern Hemisphere is the seasonal equivalent of September in the Northern Hemisphere.
The name of March comes from ancient Rome, when March was the first month of the year and named Martius after Mars, the Roman god of war.

**Revolution**

A Revolution is a fundamental change in power or organizational structures that takes place in a relatively short period of time. Aristotle described two types of political Revolution

· Complete change from one constitution to another
· Modification of an existing constitution.
Revolution s have occurred through human history and vary widely in terms of methods, duration, and motivating ideology.

**April**

April Â·) is the fourth month of the year in the Gregorian Calendar, and one of four months with a length of 30 days. April was originally the second month of the Roman calendar, before January and February were added by King Numa Pompilius about 700 BC. It became the fourth month of the calendar year (the year when twelve months are displayed in order) during the time of the decemvirs about 450 BC, when it also was given 29 days. The derivation of the name is uncertain.

| | |
|---|---|
| Party | A Party is a gathering of people who have been invited by a host for the purposes of socializing, conversation, and recreation. A Party will typically feature food and beverages, and often music and dancing as well.<br>Some parties are held in honor of a specific person, day, or event (e.g., a birthday Party, a Super Bowl Party, or a St. Patrick"s Day Party). |
| Social Democratic Party | The Social Democratic Party (Romanian: Partidul Social Democrat, PSD) is a major political party of Romania. It can be loosely classified as a center-left party, although the right-left division in Romania is quite blurred. After the 2008 Romanian legislative elections the party entered in coalition with the Democratic Liberal Party (PD-L) and formed a government led by Emil Boc, the president of the PD-L. Previously, from 2005 to 2008, the PSD was an opposition party, after it lost the 2004 legislative election to the now-defunct Justice and Truth Alliance, comprising the National Liberal Party and Democratic Party. |
| Constituent Assembly | A Constituent assembly is a body composed for the purpose of drafting or adopting a constitution. Unlike forms of constitution-making in which a constitution is unilaterally imposed by a sovereign lawmaker, the Constituent assembly creates a constitution through "internally imposed" actions, in that members of the Constituent assembly are themselves citizens, but not necessarily the rulers, of the country for which they are creating a constitution. As described by Columbia University Social Sciences Professor John Elster:<br>Constitutions arise in a number of different ways. |
| Communist Party | A political party described as a Communist Party includes those that advocate the application of the social principles of communism through a communist form of government. The name originates from the 1848 tract Manifesto of the Communist Party by Karl Marx, Friedrich Engels. The Leninist concept of a Communist Party encompasses a larger political system and includes not only an ideological orientation but also a wide set of organizational policies. |
| Empire | The term Empire derives from the Latin imperium. Politically, an Empire is a geographically extensive group of states and peoples united and ruled either by a monarch (emperor, empress) or an oligarchy. Geopolitically, the term Empire has denoted very different, territorially-extreme states -- at the strong end, the extensive Spanish Empire and the British Empire (19th c.), at the weak end, the Holy Roman Empire (8th c.-19th c.), in its Medieval and early-modern forms, and the Byzantine Empire (15th c.), that was a direct continuation of the Roman Empire, that, in its final century of existence, was more a city-state than a territorial Empire. |
| Ottoman | The state of the Ottomans which began as part of the Anatolian Seljuk Sultanate and became an independent Empire, has been known historically by different names at different periods and in various languages. This page surveys the history of these names and their usage.<br><br>· Modern Turkish: OsmanlÄ± BeyliÄŸi;<br>The first declaration of statehood happened under Osman I. |

· Ä€l-e Uá'mÄ  n

· Medieval Latin: Turchia
· Medieval Latin: Imperium Turcicum
· English: Turkey ; the current use of the name Turkey refers to the Republic of Turkey which succeeded the Ottoman Empire in 1923
· English: Turkish Empire, Ottoman Empire, Osmanic Empire, Osmanian Empire
· Ottoman Turkish/Persian: Ø¯Ù'Ù„Øª Ø¹Ù„ÙŠÙ‡ Ø'Ø«Ù…اØ§Ù†ÙŠÙ‡ Devlet-i Âliye-yi Osmâniyye
· Ottoman Turkish/Persian: Devlet-i Âliye (The Sublime State)
· Ottoman Turkish/Persian: Devlet-i Ebed-Müddet
· Ottoman Turkish/Persian: Memâlik-i Mahrûse (The Well-Protected Domains)
· Ottoman Turkish/Persian: Memâlik-i Mahrûse-i Osmanî
· Modern Turkish: OsmanlÄ± Ä°mparatorluÄŸu (Ottoman Empire),
· Arabic: Ø§Ù„Ø¯ÙˆÙ„Ø©Ù  Ø§Ù„Ø¹Ù„ÙŠØ©Ù  Ø§Ù„Ø¹Ø«Ù…اØ§Ù†ÙŠØ©Ù  Ad-Dawlat al-Ë¤Ä€lÄ« al-Ë¤UthmÄ  nÄ«
· Bulgarian: ÐžÑ Ð¼Ð°Ð½Ñ  Ð°Ð° Ð˜Ð¼Ð¿ÐµÑ€Ð¸Ñ  (Osmanska Imperia)
· Greek: ΟθωμανικÎ® ΑυτοκρατορÎ‚α
· Armenian: Õ•Õ½Õ´Õ¡Õ¶ÕµÕ¡Õ¶ Õ¿Õ¡Õ£Õ¡Õ¾Õ¸Ö€Õ¸Ö‚Õ©ÕµÕ¸Ö‚Õ¶ (Osmanyan Kaysroutyoun)
In diplomatic circles, the Ottoman government was often referred to as the "Sublime Porte", a literal translation of the Ottoman Turkish Bâb-Ä± Âlî, which was the only gate of the imperial TopkapÄ± Palace that was open to foreigners, and where the Sultan, Grand Vizier or Viziers greeted the ambassadors.

| | |
|---|---|
| Ottoman Empire | The Ottoman Empire or Ottoman State , also known by its contemporaries as the Turkish Empire or Turkey , was an empire that lasted from 1299 to November 1, 1922 (as an imperial monarchy) or July 24, 1923 (de jure, as a state.) It was succeeded by the Republic of Turkey, which was officially proclaimed on October 29, 1923.<br>At the height of its power (16th-17th century), it spanned three continents, controlling much of Southeastern Europe, Western Asia and North Africa. |
| Austria | Austria ), officially the Republic of Austria , is a landlocked country of roughly 8.3 million people in Central Europe. It borders both Germany and the Czech Republic to the north, Slovakia and Hungary to the east, Slovenia and Italy to the south, and Switzerland and Liechtenstein to the west. The territory of Austria covers 83,872 square kilometres (32,383 sq mi), and is influenced by a temperate and alpine climate. |
| Czechoslovakia | Czechoslovakia was a sovereign state in Central Europe which existed from October 1918, when it declared its independence from the Austro-Hungarian Empire, until 1992. From 1939 to 1945 the state did not have a de facto existence, due to its forced division and partial incorporation into Germany, but the Czech government-in-exile nevertheless continued to exist during this time period while Slovakia was independent from the Czech part. On 1 January 1993 Czechoslovakia peacefully split into the Czech Republic and Slovakia. |

| | |
|---|---|
| Yugoslavia | Yugoslavia is a term that describes three political entities that existed successively on the Balkan Peninsula in Europe, during most of the 20th century.<br><br>The first country to be known by this name was the Kingdom of Yugoslavia which before 3 October 1929 was known as the Kingdom of Serbs, Croats and Slovenes. It was established on 1 December 1918 by the union of the State of Slovenes, Croats and Serbs and the Kingdom of Serbia . |
| Congress | The 2001 Congress of the Greens/Green Party USA, held at Carbondale, Illinois, was a critical event in the history of the Green Party in the United States. At the Congress, occurring July 20 to July 23, at which the G/GPUSA was to consider the Boston Proposal , a tentative "merger" agreement between it and the Association of State Green Parties (ASGP). After an intense internal organizational struggle, most of which revolved around whether or not to "accredit" various delegations (and thus grant the individuals within them voting privileges), the proposal was rejected; although 55% of the members in attendance voted to approve it (99 in favor, 81 against), the organization"s bylaws required yes votes from a "super-majority" of 66.7% of the delegates in attendance to pass. |
| Koinon | The Koinon (or "League") of Free Laconians was established in 21 BC by the Emperor Augustus, giving formal structure to a group of cities that had been associated for almost two centuries.<br><br>The Eleutherolakones (á¼˜λευθερολÎ¬κωνες, free Laconians) are first mentioned in 195 BC, after Sparta"s defeat in the Roman-Spartan War. The Roman general Titus Quinctius Flaminius placed several coastal cities of the Mani Peninsula under the protection of the Achean League, freeing them from Spartan hegemony. |
| Nation | A nation is a body of people who share a real or imagined common history, culture, language or ethnic origin, who typically inhabit a particular country or territory. The development and conceptualization of the nation is closely related to the development of modern industrial states and nationalist movements in Europe in the 18th and 19th centuries, although nationalists would trace nations into the past along an uninterrupted lines of historical narrative.<br><br>Benedict Anderson argued that nations were "imagined communities" because "the members of even the smallest nation will never know most of their fellow-members, meet them, or even hear of them, yet in the minds of each lives the image of their communion", and traced their origins back to vernacular print journalism, which by its very nature was limited with linguistic zones and addressed a common audience. |
| Roman | A Roman or civil diocese was one of the administrative divisions of the later Roman Empire, starting with the Tetrarchy. It formed the intermediate level of government, grouping several provinces and being in turn subordinated to a praetorian prefecture.<br><br>The earliest use of "diocese" as an administrative unit was in the Greek-speaking East. |

| Declaration of Independence | A Declaration of independence is an assertion of the independence of an aspiring state or states. Such places are usually declared from part or all of the territory of another nation or failed nation, or are breakaway territories from within the larger state. Not all declarations of independence were successful and resulted in independence for these regions. |
|---|---|
| Koinon | The Koinon (or "League") of Free Laconians was established in 21 BC by the Emperor Augustus, giving formal structure to a group of cities that had been associated for almost two centuries. The Eleutherolakones (á¼˜λευθερολῖˬκωνες, free Laconians) are first mentioned in 195 BC, after Sparta"s defeat in the Roman-Spartan War. The Roman general Titus Quinctius Flaminius placed several coastal cities of the Mani Peninsula under the protection of the Achean League, freeing them from Spartan hegemony. |
| Nation | A nation is a body of people who share a real or imagined common history, culture, language or ethnic origin, who typically inhabit a particular country or territory. The development and conceptualization of the nation is closely related to the development of modern industrial states and nationalist movements in Europe in the 18th and 19th centuries, although nationalists would trace nations into the past along an uninterrupted lines of historical narrative. Benedict Anderson argued that nations were "imagined communities" because "the members of even the smallest nation will never know most of their fellow-members, meet them, or even hear of them, yet in the minds of each lives the image of their communion", and traced their origins back to vernacular print journalism, which by its very nature was limited with linguistic zones and addressed a common audience. |
| France | France or ; French: [fÈ É'Ìƒs]), officially the French Republic , is a country located in Western Europe, with several overseas islands and territories located on other continents. Metropolitan France extends from the Mediterranean Sea to the English Channel and the North Sea, and from the Rhine to the Atlantic Ocean. It is often referred to as L"Hexagone ("The Hexagon") because of the geometric shape of its territory. |
| Party | A Party is a gathering of people who have been invited by a host for the purposes of socializing, conversation, and recreation. A Party will typically feature food and beverages, and often music and dancing as well. Some parties are held in honor of a specific person, day, or event (e.g., a birthday Party, a Super Bowl Party, or a St. Patrick"s Day Party). |
| Canada | CANADA is a country occupying most of northern North America, extending from the Atlantic Ocean in the east to the Pacific Ocean in the west and northward into the Arctic Ocean. It is the world"s second largest country by total area and shares the world"s longest common border with the United States to the south and northwest. The land occupied by CANADA was inhabited for millennia by various groups of Aboriginal people. |

| | |
|---|---|
| Popular Front | A Popular Front is a broad coalition of different political groupings, often made up of leftists and centrists who are united by opposition to another group (most often capitalist groups). Being very broad, they can sometimes include centrist and liberal (or "bourgeois") forces as well as socialist and communist ("working-class") groups. Popular Fronts are larger in scope than united fronts, which contain only working-class groups. |
| Colonization | Colonization, , occurs whenever any one or more species populate an area. The term, which is derived from the Latin colere, "to inhabit, cultivate, frequent, practice, tend, guard, respect," originally related to humans. However, 19th century biogeographers dominated the term to describe the activities of birds, bacteria, or plant species. |
| Revolution | A Revolution is a fundamental change in power or organizational structures that takes place in a relatively short period of time. Aristotle described two types of political Revolution<br><br>· Complete change from one constitution to another<br>· Modification of an existing constitution.<br>Revolution s have occurred through human history and vary widely in terms of methods, duration, and motivating ideology. |
| India | India, officially the Indian Empire, declared war on Germany in September 1939. The Provinces of India " href="/wiki/East_African_Campaign_(World_War_II)">East African Campaign, Western Desert Campaign and the Italian Campaign. At the height of the World War, more than 2.5 million Indian troops were fighting Axis forces around the globe. |
| Nigeria | Nigeria , officially the Federal Republic of Nigeria, is a federal constitutional republic comprising thirty-six states and one Federal Capital Territory. The country is located in West Africa and shares land borders with the Republic of Benin in the west, Chad and Cameroon in the east, and Niger in the north. Its coast lies on the Gulf of Guinea, a part of the Atlantic Ocean, in the south. |
| Congress | The 2001 Congress of the Greens/Green Party USA, held at Carbondale, Illinois, was a critical event in the history of the Green Party in the United States. At the Congress, occurring July 20 to July 23, at which the G/GPUSA was to consider the Boston Proposal , a tentative "merger" agreement between it and the Association of State Green Parties (ASGP). After an intense internal organizational struggle, most of which revolved around whether or not to "accredit" various delegations (and thus grant the individuals within them voting privileges), the proposal was rejected; although 55% of the members in attendance voted to approve it (99 in favor, 81 against), the organization"s bylaws required yes votes from a "super-majority" of 66.7% of the delegates in attendance to pass. |
| World War II | During World War II, Lithuania was occupied by the Soviet Union (1940-1941), Nazi Germany , and the Soviet Union again in 1944. Resistance during this period took many forms. Significant parts of the resistance were formed by Polish and Soviet forces, some of which fought with Lithuanian collaborators. |

| | |
|---|---|
| Beer Hall Putsch | The Beer Hall Putsch was a failed attempt at revolution that occurred between the evening of 8 November and the early afternoon of 9 November 1923, when Nazi Party leader Adolf Hitler, Generalquartiermeister Erich Ludendorff, and other heads of the Kampfbund unsuccessfully tried to seize power in Munich, Bavaria, and Germany. Putsch is the German word for coup d"état. Beer halls in the early 20th century existed in most larger southern German cities, where hundreds or even thousands of people were able to gather during the evenings, drink beer and often engage in political or social debate. |
| Hall | In architecture, several things are commonly known as Halls or Halls. A Hall is fundamentally a relatively large space enclosed by a roof and walls. In the Iron Age, a mead Hall was such a simple building and was the residence of a lord and his retainers. |
| Benito Mussolini | Benito Amilcare Andrea Mussolini, KSMOM GCTE (29 July 1883 - 28 April 1945) was an Italian politician who led the National Fascist Party and is credited with being one of the key figures in the creation of Fascism. He became the Prime Minister of Italy in 1922 and began using the title Il Duce by 1925. After 1936, his official title was "His Excellency Benito Mussolini, Head of Government, Duce of Fascism, and Founder of the Empire". |
| Law | The great end, for which men entered into society, was to secure their property. That right is preserved sacred and incommunicable in all instances, where it has not been taken away or abridged by some public Law for the good of the whole ... If no excuse can be found or produced, the silence of the books is an authority against the defendant, and the plaintiff must have judgment. |
| Italy | Italy (Italian: Italia), officially the Italian Republic (Italian: Repubblica Italiana), is a country located on the Italian Peninsula in Southern Europe and on the two largest islands in the Mediterranean Sea, Sicily and Sardinia. Italy shares its northern, Alpine boundary with France, Switzerland, Austria and Slovenia. The independent states of San Marino and the Vatican City are enclaves within the Italian Peninsula, and Campione d"Italia is an Italian exclave in Switzerland. |
| Republic | A Republic is a form of government in which the head of state is not a monarch and the people (or at least a part of its people) have an impact on its government. The word "Republic" is derived from the Latin phrase res publica which can be translated as "public affairs". Both modern and ancient Republics vary widely in their ideology and composition. |
| Adolf Hitler | Adolf Hitler was an Austrian-born German politician and the leader of the National Socialist German Workers Party , popularly known as the Nazi Party. He was the ruler of Germany from 1933 to 1945, serving as chancellor from 1933 to 1945 and as head of state (Führer und Reichskanzler) from 1934 to 1945. A decorated veteran of World War I, Hitler joined the Nazi Party (DAP) in 1919 and became leader of NSDAP in 1921. |

| | |
|---|---|
| Nazi Germany | Nazi Germany and the Third Reich are the common English names for Germany between 1933 and 1945, while it was led by Adolf Hitler and the National Socialist German Worker"s Party . The name Third Reich (Drittes Reich, "Third Reich") refers to the state as the successor to the Holy Roman Empire of the Middle Ages and the German Empire of 1871-1918. In German, the state was known as Deutsches Reich until 1943, when its official name became Großdeutsches Reich . |
| Flag | The flag of former South Vietnam was designed by Emperor Thành Thái in 1890 and was used by Emperor Bảo Đại in 1948. It was the flag of the former State of Vietnam from 1949 to 1955 and later of the Republic of Vietnam from 1955 until April 30, 1975 when the south unconditionally surrendered to the north, where it was officially joined in a unified Vietnam a year later. The flag consists of a yellow field and three horizontal red stripes to and can be explained as either symbolising the unifying blood running through northern, central, and southern Vietnam, or as representing the symbol for "south" , in Daoist trigrams. |
| Purge | In history and political science, a Purge is the removal of people who are considered undesirable by those in power from a government, from another organization, or from society as a whole. Purge s can be peaceful or violent; many will end with the imprisonment or exile of those Purge d, but in some cases they will simply be removed from office. Restoring people who have been Purge d is known as rehabilitation. |
| Gleichschaltung | Gleichschaltung , meaning "coordination", "making the same", "bringing into line", is a Nazi term for the process by which the Nazi regime successively established a system of totalitarian control over the individual, and tight coordination over all aspects of society and commerce. The historian Richard J. Evans offered the term "forcible-coordination" in his most recent work on Nazi Germany. One goal of this policy was to eliminate individualism by forcing everybody to adhere to a specific doctrine and way of thinking and to control as many aspects of life as possible using an invasive police force. |
| New Order | New Order were an English musical group formed in 1980 by Bernard Sumner , Peter Hook (bass, backing vocals, electronic drums) and Stephen Morris (drums, synthesizers.) New Order were formed in the wake of the demise of their previous group Joy Division, following the suicide of vocalist Ian Curtis. They were soon joined by additional keyboardist Gillian Gilbert. |
| Austrian Empire | The Austrian Empire was a modern era successor empire founded on a remnant of the Holy Roman Empire centered on what is today"s Austria that officially lasted from 1804 to 1867. It was followed by combining the Royal House with that of Hungary creating the dual monarchy Austria-Hungary , which itself as one of the losers was dissolved at the end of World War I and broken into separate new states). The term "Austrian Empire" is also used for the Habsburg possessions before 1804, which had no official collective name, although Austria is more frequent; the term of Austria-Hungary has also been used, incorrectly. |

| | |
|---|---|
| Hitler Youth | The Hitler Youth , abbreviated HJ) was a paramilitary organization of the Nazi Party. It existed from 1922 to 1945. The HJ was the second oldest paramilitary Nazi group, founded one year after its adult counterpart, the Sturmabteilung . |
| Kristallnacht | Kristallnacht or the Night of Broken Glass was an anti-Jewish pogrom in Nazi Germany and Austria on 9 to 10 November 1938. It is often called Novemberpogrom or Reichspogromnacht in German. Kristallnacht was triggered by the assassination of German diplomat Ernst vom Rath by Herschel Grynszpan, a German-born Polish Jew. |
| Nuremberg laws | The Nuremberg Laws of 1935 were anti-Semitic laws in Nazi Germany which were introduced at the annual Nazi Party rally in Nuremberg. The laws classified people as German if all four of their grandparents were of "German or kindred blood", while people were classified as Jews if they descended from three or four Jewish grandparents. A person with one or two Jewish grandparents was a Mischling, a crossbreed, of "mixed blood". |
| Union of Soviet Socialist Republics | The Union of Soviet Socialist Republics (USSR) was a constitutionally socialist state that existed in Eurasia from 1922 to 1991. The name is a translation of the Russian: Â·), tr. Soyuz Sovetskikh Sotsialisticheskikh Respublik, abbreviated Ð¡Ð¡Ð¡Ð , SSSR. The common short name is Soviet Union, from Ð¡Ð¾Ð²ÐµÑ‚Ñ ÐºÐ¸Ð¹ Ð¡Ð¾ÑŽÐ··, Sovetskiy Soyuz. |
| Peasant | A Peasant is an agricultural worker who subsists by working a small plot of ground. The term Peasant today is sometimes used in a pejorative sense for impoverished farmers. Peasants typically make up the majority of the agricultural labour force in a Pre-industrial society, dependent on the cultivation of their land: without stockpiles of provisions they thrive or starve according to the most recent harvest. |
| Alexander | Alexander was tagus or despot of Pherae in Thessaly, and ruled from 369 BC to 358 BC. The accounts of his usurpation vary somewhat in minor points. Diodorus Siculus tells us that on the assassination of his father, the tyrant Jason of Pherae, in 370 BC, his brother Polydorus ruled for a year, and was then poisoned by Alexander, another brother. According to Xenophon, Polydorus was murdered by his brother Polyphron, and Polyphron, in 369 BC murdered by Alexander--his nephew, according to Plutarch, who relates also that Alexander worshiped the spear with which he slew his uncle as if it was a god. |
| Yugoslavia | Yugoslavia is a term that describes three political entities that existed successively on the Balkan Peninsula in Europe, during most of the 20th century. The first country to be known by this name was the Kingdom of Yugoslavia which before 3 October 1929 was known as the Kingdom of Serbs, Croats and Slovenes. It was established on 1 December 1918 by the union of the State of Slovenes, Croats and Serbs and the Kingdom of Serbia . |

| | |
|---|---|
| Greece | Greece entered World War II on 28 October 1940, when the Italian army invaded from Albania. The Greek army dealt the first victory for the Allies by defeating the invasion and pushing Mussolini"s forces back into Albania. Hitler was reluctantly forced to send his own forces to overcome Greece in April 1941, and delay the invasion of the Soviet Union by six weeks. |
| Portugal | Portugal , officially the Portuguese Republic (Portuguese: República Portuguesa), is a country on the Iberian Peninsula, member of the European Union and one of the founding members of NATO. Located in southwestern Europe, Portugal is the westernmost country of mainland Europe and is bordered by the Atlantic Ocean to the west and south and by Spain to the north and east. The Atlantic archipelagos of the Azores and Madeira are also part of Portugal.<br>The land within the borders of today"s Portuguese Republic has been continuously settled since prehistoric times. |
| Rivera | Rivera is a municipality in the district of Lugano in the canton of Ticino in Switzerland. |
| Mari | Mari (modern Tell Hariri, Syria) was an ancient Sumerian and Amorite city, located 11 kilometers north-west of the modern town of Abu Kamal on the western bank of Euphrates river, some 120 km southeast of Deir ez-Zor, Syria. It is thought to have been inhabited since the 5th millennium BC, although it flourished from 2900 BC until 1759 BC, when it was sacked by Hammurabi.<br>Mari was discovered in 1933 on the eastern flank of Syria, near the Iraqi border. |

| | |
|---|---|
| Beer Hall Putsch | The Beer Hall Putsch was a failed attempt at revolution that occurred between the evening of 8 November and the early afternoon of 9 November 1923, when Nazi Party leader Adolf Hitler, Generalquartiermeister Erich Ludendorff, and other heads of the Kampfbund unsuccessfully tried to seize power in Munich, Bavaria, and Germany. Putsch is the German word for coup d"état. Beer halls in the early 20th century existed in most larger southern German cities, where hundreds or even thousands of people were able to gather during the evenings, drink beer and often engage in political or social debate. |
| Hall | In architecture, several things are commonly known as Halls or Halls. A Hall is fundamentally a relatively large space enclosed by a roof and walls. In the Iron Age, a mead Hall was such a simple building and was the residence of a lord and his retainers. |
| Revolution | A Revolution is a fundamental change in power or organizational structures that takes place in a relatively short period of time. Aristotle described two types of political Revolution<br><br>· Complete change from one constitution to another<br>· Modification of an existing constitution.<br>Revolution s have occurred through human history and vary widely in terms of methods, duration, and motivating ideology. |
| Koinon | The Koinon (or "League") of Free Laconians was established in 21 BC by the Emperor Augustus, giving formal structure to a group of cities that had been associated for almost two centuries.<br>The Eleutherolakones ( á¼˜λευθερολÎ¬κωνες, free Laconians) are first mentioned in 195 BC, after Sparta"s defeat in the Roman-Spartan War. The Roman general Titus Quinctius Flaminius placed several coastal cities of the Mani Peninsula under the protection of the Achean League, freeing them from Spartan hegemony. |
| Nation | A nation is a body of people who share a real or imagined common history, culture, language or ethnic origin, who typically inhabit a particular country or territory. The development and conceptualization of the nation is closely related to the development of modern industrial states and nationalist movements in Europe in the 18th and 19th centuries, although nationalists would trace nations into the past along an uninterrupted lines of historical narrative.<br>Benedict Anderson argued that nations were "imagined communities" because "the members of even the smallest nation will never know most of their fellow-members, meet them, or even hear of them, yet in the minds of each lives the image of their communion", and traced their origins back to vernacular print journalism, which by its very nature was limited with linguistic zones and addressed a common audience. |
| Nazi Germany | Nazi Germany and the Third Reich are the common English names for Germany between 1933 and 1945, while it was led by Adolf Hitler and the National Socialist German Worker"s Party . The name Third Reich (Drittes Reich, "Third Reich") refers to the state as the successor to the Holy Roman Empire of the Middle Ages and the German Empire of 1871-1918. In German, the state was known as Deutsches Reich until 1943, when its official name became Großdeutsches Reich . |

| | |
|---|---|
| Anti-Comintern Pact | The Anti-Comintern Pact was concluded between Nazi Germany and the Empire of Japan on November 25, 1936 and was directed against the Communist International (Comintern) in general, and the Soviet Union in particular.<br><br>"recognizing that the aim of the Communist International, known as the Comintern, is to disintegrate and subdue existing States by all the means at its command; convinced that the toleration of interference by the Communist International in the internal affairs of the nations not only endangers their internal peace and social wellâ€'being, but is also a menace to the peace of the world desirous of coâ€'operating in the defense against Communist subversive activities"<br><br>The origins of the Anti-Comintern Pact go back to the autumn of 1935, when various German officials both within and without the Foreign Ministry were attempting to balance the competing demands upon the Reich"s foreign policy by its traditional alliance with China vs Hitler"s desire for friendship with China"s archenemy, Japan. In October 1935, the idea was mooted that an anti-Communist alliance might be able to tie in the Kuomintang regime, Japan and Germany. |
| Appeasement | Appeasement is "the policy of settling international quarrels by admitting and satisfying grievances through rational negotiation and compromise, thereby avoiding the resort to an armed conflict which would be expensive, bloody, and possibly dangerous." The term is most often applied to the foreign policy of British Prime Minister Neville Chamberlain towards Nazi Germany between 1937 and 1939. Appeasement has been the subject of debate for eighty years among academics and politicians. The historian"s assessment of Chamberlain has ranged from condemnation to the judgment that he had no alternative and acted in Britain"s best interests. |
| Austria | Austria ), officially the Republic of Austria , is a landlocked country of roughly 8.3 million people in Central Europe. It borders both Germany and the Czech Republic to the north, Slovakia and Hungary to the east, Slovenia and Italy to the south, and Switzerland and Liechtenstein to the west. The territory of Austria covers 83,872 square kilometres (32,383 sq mi), and is influenced by a temperate and alpine climate. |
| Blitzkrieg | Blitzkrieg ) is "a headline word applied retrospectively to describe a military doctrine of an all-mechanized force concentrating its attack on a small section of the enemy front then, once the latter is broken, proceeding without regard to its flank."<br><br>During the interwar period, airplane and tank technologies matured and were combined with systematic application of the German tactics of infiltration and bypassing of enemy strong points. When Germany invaded Poland in 1939, Western journalists adopted the term Blitzkrieg to describe this form of armored warfare.<br><br>"Blitzkrieg" operations worked in the German invasions of Western Europe and initial operations in the Soviet Union. |

| | |
|---|---|
| Benito Mussolini | Benito Amilcare Andrea Mussolini, KSMOM GCTE (29 July 1883 - 28 April 1945) was an Italian politician who led the National Fascist Party and is credited with being one of the key figures in the creation of Fascism. He became the Prime Minister of Italy in 1922 and began using the title Il Duce by 1925. After 1936, his official title was "His Excellency Benito Mussolini, Head of Government, Duce of Fascism, and Founder of the Empire". |
| Czechoslovakia | Czechoslovakia was a sovereign state in Central Europe which existed from October 1918, when it declared its independence from the Austro-Hungarian Empire, until 1992. From 1939 to 1945 the state did not have a de facto existence, due to its forced division and partial incorporation into Germany, but the Czech government-in-exile nevertheless continued to exist during this time period while Slovakia was independent from the Czech part. On 1 January 1993 Czechoslovakia peacefully split into the Czech Republic and Slovakia. |
| Sudetenland | Sudetenland (Czech and Slovak: Sudety, Polish: Kraj Sudetów) is the German name used in English in the first half of the 20th century for the western regions of Czechoslovakia inhabited mostly by ethnic Germans, specifically the border areas of Bohemia, Moravia, and those parts of Silesia associated with Bohemia. The German inhabitants were called Sudeten Germans . The German minority in Slovakia, the Carpathian Germans, is not included in this ethnic category. |
| New Order | New Order were an English musical group formed in 1980 by Bernard Sumner , Peter Hook (bass, backing vocals, electronic drums) and Stephen Morris (drums, synthesizers.) New Order were formed in the wake of the demise of their previous group Joy Division, following the suicide of vocalist Ian Curtis. They were soon joined by additional keyboardist Gillian Gilbert. |
| Dutch East Indies | The Dutch East Indies, or Netherlands East Indies, (Dutch: Nederlands-Indië; Indonesian: Hindia-Belanda) was the Dutch colony that became modern Indonesia following World War II. It was formed from the nationalised colonies of the former Dutch East India Company that came under the administration of the Netherlands in 1800. During the nineteenth century, Dutch possessions in the archipelago and its hegemony were expanded, reaching their greatest extent in the early twentieth century. Following the World War II Japanese occupation, Indonesian nationalists declared Indonesian independence in 1945. |
| France | France or ; French: [fʁɑ̃s]), officially the French Republic , is a country located in Western Europe, with several overseas islands and territories located on other continents. Metropolitan France extends from the Mediterranean Sea to the English Channel and the North Sea, and from the Rhine to the Atlantic Ocean. It is often referred to as L"Hexagone ("The Hexagon") because of the geometric shape of its territory. |

Vichy (Occitan: Vichèi) is a commune in the department of Allier in Auvergne in central France. It is known as a spa and resort town. It was the de facto capital of Vichy France during the World War II Nazi German occupation from 1940 to 1944.

| Vichy | | Commune of Vichy |
|---|---|---|

Town Hall
Location

**Administration**

| | |
|---|---|
| Country | France |
| Region | Auvergne |
| Department | Allier |
| Arrondissement | Vichy |
| Intercommunality | Vichy Val d"Allier |
| Mayor | Claude Malhuret |

**Statistics**

| | |
|---|---|
| Elevation | 249 m (820 ft) avg. |
| Land area[1] | 5.85 km$^2$ (2.26 sq mi) |
| Population[2] | 26,528 (1999) |
| - Density | 4,535 /km$^2$ (11,750 /sq mi) |

Miscellaneous

| | |
|---|---|
| INSEE/Postal code | 03310/ 03200 |

[1] French Land Register data, which excludes lakes, ponds, glaciers > 1 km$^2$ and river estuaries.

[2] Population sans doubles comptes: residents of multiple communes (e.g., students and military personnel) only counted once.

| Vichy France | Vichy France or the Vichy regime are the common terms used to describe the government of France from July 1940 to August 1944. This government, which succeeded the Third Republic, officially called itself the French State , in contrast with the previous designation, "French Republic." Marshal Philippe Pétain proclaimed the government following the military defeat of France by Nazi Germany during World War II and the vote by the National Assembly on 10 July 1940. This vote granted extraordinary powers to Pétain, the last Président du Conseil (Prime Minister) of the Third Republic, who then took the additional title Chef de l"État Français . |
|---|---|

| | |
|---|---|
| Greece | Greece entered World War II on 28 October 1940, when the Italian army invaded from Albania. The Greek army dealt the first victory for the Allies by defeating the invasion and pushing Mussolini"s forces back into Albania. Hitler was reluctantly forced to send his own forces to overcome Greece in April 1941, and delay the invasion of the Soviet Union by six weeks. |
| Union of Soviet Socialist Republics | The Union of Soviet Socialist Republics (USSR) was a constitutionally socialist state that existed in Eurasia from 1922 to 1991. The name is a translation of the Russian: Â·), tr. Soyuz Sovetskikh Sotsialisticheskikh Respublik, abbreviated Ð¡Ð¡Ð¡Ð , SSSR. The common short name is Soviet Union, from Ð¡Ð¾Ð²ÐµÑ‚Ñ  ÐºÐ¸Ð¹ Ð¡Ð¾ÑŽÐ··, Sovetskiy Soyuz. |
| Yugoslavia | Yugoslavia is a term that describes three political entities that existed successively on the Balkan Peninsula in Europe, during most of the 20th century.<br>The first country to be known by this name was the Kingdom of Yugoslavia which before 3 October 1929 was known as the Kingdom of Serbs, Croats and Slovenes. It was established on 1 December 1918 by the union of the State of Slovenes, Croats and Serbs and the Kingdom of Serbia . |
| Invasion of Yugoslavia | The Invasion of Yugoslavia (code-name Directive n. 25), also known as the April War (Croatian: Travanjski rat, Serbian/Bosnian: Aprilski rat, Slovene: aprilska vojna), was the Axis Powers" attack on Kingdom of Yugoslavia on April 6, 1941 during World War II. The invasion ended with the unconditional surrender of the Royal Yugoslav Army on April 17, 1941, the occupation of the region by the Axis and the creation of the Independent State of Croatia (Nezavisna DrÃ¾ava Hrvatska, or NDH).<br>In October 1940, Fascist Italy had attacked Greece only to be forced back into Albania. |
| Axis powers | The Axis powers comprised the countries that were opposed to the Allies during World War II. The three major Axis powers--Germany, Italy, and Japan--were part of a military alliance on the signing of the Tripartite Pact in September 1940, which officially founded the Axis powers. At their zenith, the Axis powers ruled empires that dominated large parts of Europe, Africa, East and Southeast Asia and the Pacific Ocean, but World War II ended with their total defeat. Like the Allies, membership of the Axis was fluid, and some nations entered and later left the Axis during the course of the war. |
| Grand Alliance | The Grand Alliance was a European coalition, consisting (at various times) of Austria, Bavaria, Brandenburg, England, the Holy Roman Empire, the Palatinate of the Rhine, Portugal, Savoy, Saxony, Spain, Sweden, and the United Provinces. The organization, which was founded in 1686 as the League of Augsburg, was known as the "Grand Alliance" after England joined the League .<br>The League was officially formed by Emperor Leopold I, acting upon the advice of William III of Orange. |
| Empire | The term Empire derives from the Latin imperium. Politically, an Empire is a geographically extensive group of states and peoples united and ruled either by a monarch (emperor, empress) or an oligarchy. Geopolitically, the term Empire has denoted very different, territorially-extreme states -- at the strong end, the extensive Spanish Empire and the British Empire (19th c.)., at the weak end, the Holy Roman Empire (8th c.-19th c.)., in its Medieval and early-modern forms, and the Byzantine Empire (15th c.), that was a direct continuation of the Roman Empire, that, in its final century of existence, was more a city-state than a territorial Empire. |

| | |
|---|---|
| Adolf Hitler | Adolf Hitler was an Austrian-born German politician and the leader of the National Socialist German Workers Party , popularly known as the Nazi Party. He was the ruler of Germany from 1933 to 1945, serving as chancellor from 1933 to 1945 and as head of state (Führer und Reichskanzler) from 1934 to 1945. <br><br> A decorated veteran of World War I, Hitler joined the Nazi Party (DAP) in 1919 and became leader of NSDAP in 1921. |
| White Rose | The White Rose was a non-violent/intellectual resistance group in Nazi Germany, consisting of students from the University of Munich and their philosophy professor. The group became known for an anonymous leaflet campaign, lasting from June 1942 until February 1943, that called for active opposition to German dictator Adolf Hitler"s regime. <br><br> The six core members of the group were arrested by the Gestapo and they were executed by decapitation in 1943. |
| Assassination | Assassination, the murder of an opponent or well-known public figure, is one of the oldest tools of power struggles, as well as the expression of certain psychopathic disorders. It dates back to the earliest governments and tribal structures of the world. Leon Czolgosz shoots US President William McKinley in 1901, with a concealed revolver. <br><br> Chanakya (c. |
| Hitler Youth | The Hitler Youth , abbreviated HJ) was a paramilitary organization of the Nazi Party. It existed from 1922 to 1945. The HJ was the second oldest paramilitary Nazi group, founded one year after its adult counterpart, the Sturmabteilung . |
| Final Solution | The Final Solution was Nazi Germany"s plan and execution of its systematic genocide against European Jewry during World War II, resulting in the final, most deadly phase of the Holocaust. Heinrich Himmler was the chief architect of the plan, and the German Nazi leader Adolf Hitler termed it: "the Final Solution of the Jewish question" . <br><br> Mass killings of about one million Jews occurred before the plans of the Final Solution were fully implemented in 1942, but it was only with the decision to eradicate the entire Jewish population that the extermination camps were built and industrialized mass slaughter of Jews began in earnest. |
| Austria-Hungary | Austria-Hungary the Dual Monarchy or the k.u.k Monarchy, was a state in Central Europe ruled by the House of Habsburg, constitutionally a monarchic union between the crowns of the Austrian Empire and the Kingdom of Hungary. The state was a result of the Ausgleich or Compromise of 1867, under which the Austrian Habsburgs agreed to share power with a separate Hungarian government, dividing the territory of the former Austrian Empire between them. The Dual Monarchy existed for 51 years until 1918, when it dissolved following military defeat in the First World War. |
| Office of Price Administration | The Office of Price Administration (OPA) was established within the Office for Emergency Management of the United States Government by Executive Order 8875 on August 28, 1941. The functions of the OPA were originally to stabilize prices (price controls) and rents after the outbreak of World War II. |

President Franklin D. Roosevelt revived the Advisory Commission to World War I Council on National Defense on May 29, 1940 to include Price Stabilization and Consumer Protection Divisions. Both divisions merged to become the Office of Price Administration and Civilian Supply (OPACS) within the Office for Emergency Management by Executive Order 8734, April 11, 1941.

**Peasant**

A Peasant is an agricultural worker who subsists by working a small plot of ground. The term Peasant today is sometimes used in a pejorative sense for impoverished farmers.

Peasants typically make up the majority of the agricultural labour force in a Pre-industrial society, dependent on the cultivation of their land: without stockpiles of provisions they thrive or starve according to the most recent harvest.

**Project**

A Project in business and science is a collaborative enterprise, frequently involving research or design, that is carefully planned to achieve a particular aim.

The word Project comes from the Latin word Projectum from the Latin verb proicere, "to throw something forwards" which in turn comes from pro-, which denotes something that precedes the action of the next part of the word in time and iacere, "to throw". The word "Project" thus actually originally meant "something that comes before anything else happens".

**Kamikaze**

The Kamikaze ) were suicide attacks by military aviators from the Empire of Japan against Allied naval vessels in the closing stages of the Pacific campaign of World War II, designed to destroy as many warships as possible.

Kamikaze pilots would attempt to intentionally crash their aircraft - often laden with explosives, bombs, torpedoes and full fuel tanks - into Allied ships. The aircraft"s normal functions, to deliver torpedoes or bombs or shoot down other aircraft, were put aside, and the planes were converted to what were essentially manned missiles, in a desperate attempt to reap the benefits of greatly increased accuracy and payload over that of normal bombs.

**J. Robert Oppenheimer**

J. Robert Oppenheimer (April 22, 1904 - February 18, 1967) was an American theoretical physicist and professor of physics at the University of California, Berkeley. He is best known for his role as the scientific director of the Manhattan Project, the World War II effort to develop the first nuclear weapons at the secret Los Alamos National Laboratory in New Mexico. For this reason he is remembered as "The Father of the Atomic Bomb".

**Philippines**

The Philippines (Tagalog: Pilipinas [pɛ ᵃlɛ ᵃɛˆpinɛ s]) officially known as the Republic of the Philippines, is a country in Southeast Asia with Manila as its capital city. It comprises 7,107 islands in the western Pacific Ocean.

The Philippines is the world"s 12th most populous country, with an estimated population of about 92 million people.

**World War II**

During World War II, Lithuania was occupied by the Soviet Union (1940-1941), Nazi Germany , and the Soviet Union again in 1944. Resistance during this period took many forms. Significant parts of the resistance were formed by Polish and Soviet forces, some of which fought with Lithuanian collaborators.

| Tehran Conference | The Tehran Conference was the meeting of Joseph Stalin, Franklin D. Roosevelt and Winston Churchill between November 28 and December 1, 1943, most of which was held at the Soviet Embassy in Tehran, Iran. It was the first World War II conference among the Big Three (the Soviet Union, the United States, and the United Kingdom) in which Stalin was present. It succeeded the Cairo Conference and was followed by the Yalta Conference and Potsdam Conference. |
| --- | --- |
| Potsdam Conference | The Potsdam Conference was held at Cecilienhof, the home of Crown Prince Wilhelm Hohenzollern, in Potsdam, occupied Germany, from 16 July to 2 August 1945. Participants were the Soviet Union, the United Kingdom, and the United States. The three nations were represented by Communist Party General Secretary Joseph Stalin, Prime Ministers Winston Churchill and later Clement Attlee, and President Harry S. Truman. |

| | |
|---|---|
| World War II | During World War II, Lithuania was occupied by the Soviet Union (1940-1941), Nazi Germany , and the Soviet Union again in 1944. Resistance during this period took many forms. Significant parts of the resistance were formed by Polish and Soviet forces, some of which fought with Lithuanian collaborators. |
| Greece | Greece entered World War II on 28 October 1940, when the Italian army invaded from Albania. The Greek army dealt the first victory for the Allies by defeating the invasion and pushing Mussolini"s forces back into Albania. Hitler was reluctantly forced to send his own forces to overcome Greece in April 1941, and delay the invasion of the Soviet Union by six weeks. |
| Koinon | The Koinon (or "League") of Free Laconians was established in 21 BC by the Emperor Augustus, giving formal structure to a group of cities that had been associated for almost two centuries. The Eleutherolakones (ἀ¼¨λευθερολῖ¬κωνες, free Laconians) are first mentioned in 195 BC, after Sparta"s defeat in the Roman-Spartan War. The Roman general Titus Quinctius Flaminius placed several coastal cities of the Mani Peninsula under the protection of the Achean League, freeing them from Spartan hegemony. |
| Communist Party | A political party described as a Communist Party includes those that advocate the application of the social principles of communism through a communist form of government. The name originates from the 1848 tract Manifesto of the Communist Party by Karl Marx, Friedrich Engels. The Leninist concept of a Communist Party encompasses a larger political system and includes not only an ideological orientation but also a wide set of organizational policies. |
| Denazification | Denazification was an Allied initiative to rid German and Austrian society, culture, press, economy, judiciary, and politics of any remnants of the Nazi regime. It was carried out specifically by removing those involved from positions of influence and by disbanding or rendering impotent the organizations associated with it. The program of Denazification was launched after the end of the Second World War and was solidified by the Potsdam Agreement. |
| Revolution | A Revolution is a fundamental change in power or organizational structures that takes place in a relatively short period of time. Aristotle described two types of political Revolution<br><br>· Complete change from one constitution to another<br>· Modification of an existing constitution.<br>Revolution s have occurred through human history and vary widely in terms of methods, duration, and motivating ideology. |
| Air | The Earth"s atmosphere is a layer of gases surrounding the planet Earth that is retained by Earth"s gravity. The atmosphere protects life on Earth by absorbing ultraviolet solar radiation, warming the surface through heat retention (greenhouse effect), and reducing temperature extremes between day and night. Dry Air contains roughly (by volume) 78.08% nitrogen, 20.95% oxygen, 0.93% argon, 0.038% carbon dioxide, and trace amounts of other gases. |

| | |
|---|---|
| German Democratic Republic | The German Democratic Republic was a self-declared socialist state (but commonly referred to in the West as a communist state) that originated from the Soviet Zone of occupied Germany and the Soviet sector of occupied Berlin. The German Democratic Republic existed from 7 October 1949 until 3 October 1990, when its re-established states acceded to the adjacent Federal Republic of Germany, thus producing the current form of Germany. During its existence, the German Democratic Republic was a member of the Eastern Bloc of eastern European nations that were aligned with the Soviet Union . |
| Nation | A nation is a body of people who share a real or imagined common history, culture, language or ethnic origin, who typically inhabit a particular country or territory. The development and conceptualization of the nation is closely related to the development of modern industrial states and nationalist movements in Europe in the 18th and 19th centuries, although nationalists would trace nations into the past along an uninterrupted lines of historical narrative. |
| | Benedict Anderson argued that nations were "imagined communities" because "the members of even the smallest nation will never know most of their fellow-members, meet them, or even hear of them, yet in the minds of each lives the image of their communion", and traced their origins back to vernacular print journalism, which by its very nature was limited with linguistic zones and addressed a common audience. |
| Force | In physics, a Force is any external agent that causes a change in the motion of a free body, or that causes stress in a fixed body. It can also be described by intuitive concepts such as a push or pull that can cause an object with mass to change its velocity , i.e., to accelerate, or which can cause a flexible object to deform. Force has both magnitude and direction, making it a vector quantity. |
| France | France or ; French: [fÊ É'Ìƒs]), officially the French Republic , is a country located in Western Europe, with several overseas islands and territories located on other continents. Metropolitan France extends from the Mediterranean Sea to the English Channel and the North Sea, and from the Rhine to the Atlantic Ocean. It is often referred to as L"Hexagone ("The Hexagon") because of the geometric shape of its territory. |
| Fulgencio Batista | Fulgencio Batista y Zaldívar (January 16, 1901 - August 6, 1973) was a Cuban general, President, and U.S.-backed dictator. He served as the leader of Cuba from 1933-1944, and 1952-1959, before being overthrown as a result of the Cuban Revolution. |
| | Fulgencio was born in Banes, Cuba in 1901 to Belisario Batista Palermo and Carmela Zaldívar González, Cubans who fought for independence from Spain. |
| African National Congress | The African National Congress has been South Africa"s governing party, supported by its tripartite alliance with the Congress of South African Trade Unions (COSATU) and the South African Communist Party (SACP), since the establishment of non-racial democracy in April 1994. It defines itself as a "disciplined force of the left". Members founded the organization as the South African Native National Congress (SANNC) on 8 January 1912 in Bloemfontein to increase the rights of the black South African population. |

| | |
|---|---|
| Angola | Angola, officially the Republic of Angola , is a country in south-central Africa bordered by Namibia on the south, Democratic Republic of the Congo on the north, and Zambia on the east; its west coast is on the Atlantic Ocean. The exclave province of Cabinda has a border with the Republic of the Congo and the Democratic Republic of the Congo. Angola was a Portuguese overseas territory from the 16th century to 1975. |
| Nigeria | Nigeria , officially the Federal Republic of Nigeria, is a federal constitutional republic comprising thirty-six states and one Federal Capital Territory. The country is located in West Africa and shares land borders with the Republic of Benin in the west, Chad and Cameroon in the east, and Niger in the north. Its coast lies on the Gulf of Guinea, a part of the Atlantic Ocean, in the south. |
| Portugal | Portugal , officially the Portuguese Republic (Portuguese: República Portuguesa), is a country on the Iberian Peninsula, member of the European Union and one of the founding members of NATO. Located in southwestern Europe, Portugal is the westernmost country of mainland Europe and is bordered by the Atlantic Ocean to the west and south and by Spain to the north and east. The Atlantic archipelagos of the Azores and Madeira are also part of Portugal. The land within the borders of today"s Portuguese Republic has been continuously settled since prehistoric times. |
| United Arab Republic | The United Arab Republic , often abbreviated as the U.A.R., was a union between Egypt, and Syria. The union began in 1958 and existed until 1961 when Syria seceded from the union. Egypt continued to be known officially as the "United Arab Republic" until 1971. |
| Dutch East Indies | The Dutch East Indies, or Netherlands East Indies, (Dutch: Nederlands-Indië; Indonesian: Hindia-Belanda) was the Dutch colony that became modern Indonesia following World War II. It was formed from the nationalised colonies of the former Dutch East India Company that came under the administration of the Netherlands in 1800. During the nineteenth century, Dutch possessions in the archipelago and its hegemony were expanded, reaching their greatest extent in the early twentieth century. Following the World War II Japanese occupation, Indonesian nationalists declared Indonesian independence in 1945. |
| Empire | The term Empire derives from the Latin imperium. Politically, an Empire is a geographically extensive group of states and peoples united and ruled either by a monarch (emperor, empress) or an oligarchy. Geopolitically, the term Empire has denoted very different, territorially-extreme states -- at the strong end, the extensive Spanish Empire and the British Empire (19th c.)., at the weak end, the Holy Roman Empire (8th c.-19th c.)., in its Medieval and early-modern forms, and the Byzantine Empire (15th c.), that was a direct continuation of the Roman Empire, that, in its final century of existence, was more a city-state than a territorial Empire. |
| India | India, officially the Indian Empire, declared war on Germany in September 1939. The Provinces of India " href="/wiki/East_African_Campaign_(World_War_II)">East African Campaign, Western Desert Campaign and the Italian Campaign. At the height of the World War, more than 2.5 million Indian troops were fighting Axis forces around the globe. |

| Indian National Congress | From its foundation on 28 December 1885 till the time of independence of India on August 15, 1947, the Indian National Congress was the largest and most prominent Indian public organization, and central and defining influence of the Indian Independence Movement. |
|---|---|
| | Although initially and primarily a political body, the Congress transformed itself into a national vehicle for social reform and human upliftment. And the Congress"s foundations in democracy and multiculturalism helped make India a consistently democratic and free nation. |

| Burma Road | The Burma Road is a road linking Burma with China. Its terminals are Kunming, Yunnan and Lashio, Burma. When it was built, Burma was a British colony. |
|---|---|

| Sukarno | Sukarno, born Kusno Sosrodihardjo (6 June 1901 - 21 June 1970) was the first President of Indonesia. He helped the country win its independence from the Netherlands and was President from 1945 to 1967, presiding with mixed success over the country"s turbulent transition to independence. Sukarno was forced out of power by one of his generals, Suharto, who formally became President in March 1967. |
|---|---|

| Alexander | Alexander was tagus or despot of Pherae in Thessaly, and ruled from 369 BC to 358 BC. |
|---|---|
| | The accounts of his usurpation vary somewhat in minor points. Diodorus Siculus tells us that on the assassination of his father, the tyrant Jason of Pherae, in 370 BC, his brother Polydorus ruled for a year, and was then poisoned by Alexander, another brother. According to Xenophon, Polydorus was murdered by his brother Polyphron, and Polyphron, in 369 BC murdered by Alexander--his nephew, according to Plutarch, who relates also that Alexander worshiped the spear with which he slew his uncle as if it was a god. |

| Czechoslovakia | Czechoslovakia was a sovereign state in Central Europe which existed from October 1918, when it declared its independence from the Austro-Hungarian Empire, until 1992. From 1939 to 1945 the state did not have a de facto existence, due to its forced division and partial incorporation into Germany, but the Czech government-in-exile nevertheless continued to exist during this time period while Slovakia was independent from the Czech part. On 1 January 1993 Czechoslovakia peacefully split into the Czech Republic and Slovakia. |
|---|---|

| Ottoman | The state of the Ottomans which began as part of the Anatolian Seljuk Sultanate and became an independent Empire, has been known historically by different names at different periods and in various languages. This page surveys the history of these names and their usage. |
|---|---|
| | · Modern Turkish: Osmanlı Beyliği; The first declaration of statehood happened under Osman I. |
| | · Ä€l-e Uá'mÄ n |

· Medieval Latin: Turchia
· Medieval Latin: Imperium Turcicum
· English: Turkey ; the current use of the name Turkey refers to the Republic of Turkey which succeeded the Ottoman Empire in 1923
· English: Turkish Empire, Ottoman Empire, Osmanic Empire, Osmanian Empire
· Ottoman Turkish/Persian: Ø¯ÙˆÙ„Øª Ø¹Ù„ÛŒÙ‡ Ø¹Ø«Ù…Ø§Ù†ÛŒÙ‡ Devlet-i Âliye-yi Osmâniyye
· Ottoman Turkish/Persian: Devlet-i Âliye (The Sublime State)
· Ottoman Turkish/Persian: Devlet-i Ebed-Müddet
· Ottoman Turkish/Persian: Memâlik-i Mahrûse (The Well-Protected Domains)
· Ottoman Turkish/Persian: Memâlik-i Mahrûse-i Osmanî
· Modern Turkish: OsmanlÄ± Ä°mparatorluÄŸu (Ottoman Empire),
· Arabic: Ø§Ù„Ø¯ÙˆÙ„Ø©Ù Ø§Ù„Ø¹Ù„ÛŒØ©Ù Ø§Ù„Ø¹Ø«Ù…Ø§Ù†ÛŒØ©Ù Ad-Dawlat al-Ë¤Ä€lÄ« al-Ë¤UthmÄ nÄ«
· Bulgarian: ÐžÑ Ð¼Ð°Ð½ÑÐºÐ° Ð¸Ð¼Ð¿ÐµÑ€Ð¸Ñ (Osmanska Imperia)
· Greek: ÎŸÎ¸Ï‰Î¼Î±Î½Î¹ÎºÎ® Î‘Ï…Ï„Î¿ÎºÏ€Î±Ï„Î¿Ï Î± α
· Armenian: Õ•Õ½Õ´Õ¡Õ¶Õ¥Õ¡Õ¶ Ô¿Õ¡Õµ½Õ¼Õ¸Ö‚Õ©Õ¸Ö‚Õ¶ (Osmanyan Kaysroutyoun)
In diplomatic circles, the Ottoman government was often referred to as the "Sublime Porte", a literal translation of the Ottoman Turkish Bâb-Ä± Âlî, which was the only gate of the imperial TopkapÄ± Palace that was open to foreigners, and where the Sultan, Grand Vizier or Viziers greeted the ambassadors.

| | |
|---|---|
| Social Democratic Party | The Social Democratic Party (Romanian: Partidul Social Democrat, PSD) is a major political party of Romania. It can be loosely classified as a center-left party, although the right-left division in Romania is quite blurred. After the 2008 Romanian legislative elections the party entered in coalition with the Democratic Liberal Party (PD-L) and formed a government led by Emil Boc, the president of the PD-L. Previously, from 2005 to 2008, the PSD was an opposition party, after it lost the 2004 legislative election to the now-defunct Justice and Truth Alliance, comprising the National Liberal Party and Democratic Party. |
| Canada | CANADA is a country occupying most of northern North America, extending from the Atlantic Ocean in the east to the Pacific Ocean in the west and northward into the Arctic Ocean. It is the world"s second largest country by total area and shares the world"s longest common border with the United States to the south and northwest. The land occupied by CANADA was inhabited for millennia by various groups of Aboriginal people. |
| Scientific Revolution | In the history of science, the Scientific revolution was a period when new ideas in physics, astronomy, biology, human anatomy, chemistry, and other sciences led to a rejection of doctrines that had prevailed from Ancient Greece through the Middle Ages, and laid the foundation of modern science. According to the majority of scholars, the Scientific revolution began with the publication of two works that changed the course of science in 1543 and continued through the late 17th century: Nicolaus Copernicus"s De revolutionibus orbium coelestium (On the Revolutions of the Heavenly Spheres) and Andreas Vesalius"s De humani corporis fabrica (On the Fabric of the Human body.) |

Philosopher and historian Alexandre Koyré coined the term Scientific revolution in 1939 to describe this epoch.

**Italy**

Italy (Italian: Italia), officially the Italian Republic (Italian: Repubblica Italiana), is a country located on the Italian Peninsula in Southern Europe and on the two largest islands in the Mediterranean Sea, Sicily and Sardinia. Italy shares its northern, Alpine boundary with France, Switzerland, Austria and Slovenia. The independent states of San Marino and the Vatican City are enclaves within the Italian Peninsula, and Campione d"Italia is an Italian exclave in Switzerland.

**African Americans**

Due to the prevailing social climate that existed in the United States after World War II, one in which racism was a prominent factor, African Americans did not benefit from the provisions of the G. I. Bill of Rights as much as their white counterparts. Though the bill did provide a more level playing field than the one blacks faced during Reconstruction, this is not saying much. Representative John Elliott Rankin, an economic liberal who was also an avid segregationist and racist, sponsored the bill in the United States House of Representatives.

**Civil rights movement**

The Civil rights movement was a worldwide political movement for equality before the law occurring between approximately 1950 and 1980. It was accompanied by much civil unrest and popular rebellion. The process was long and tenuous in many countries, and most of these movements did not achieve or fully achieve their objectives.

**Republic of the Seven United Netherlands**

The Republic of the Seven United Netherlands (or "of the Seven United Provinces") was a European republic between 1581 and 1795, in about the same location as the modern Kingdom of the Netherlands, which is the successor state.

Before 1581, the area of the Low Countries consisted of a number of duchies, counties, and independent bishoprics, some but not all of them part of the Holy Roman Empire. Today that area is divided between the Netherlands, Belgium, Luxembourg and parts of France and Germany.

**United States**

The United States retained a fully civilian democratic government structure throughout World War II. Certain expediencies were taken within the existing structure of the Federal government, such as conscription and other violations of civil liberties, and the incarceration and later dispersal of Japanese-Americans. Still, elections were held as scheduled in 1944.

The United States entered World War II with the same Administration that had been at the helm of the nation since 1932, that of Franklin Delano Roosevelt.

**Liberal Party**

Liberal Party is the name of dozens of political parties around the world. It usually designates a party that is ideologically liberal, meaning that they advocate individual rights and civil liberties, and sometimes left wing, meaning that they are reliant on governmental solutions to social and economic problems. There are also some Liberal Parties which subscribe to classical liberalism and therefore support a mostly unregulated free market.

**Riot**

A Riot is a form of civil disorder characterized by disorganized groups lashing out in a sudden and intense rash of violence against people or property. While individuals may attempt to lead or control a Riot, Riots are typically chaotic and exhibit herd behavior.

Riots often occur in reaction to a perceived grievance or out of dissent.

| Liberation movement | A Liberation movement is an organization fighting a rebellion against a colonial power, often seeking independence based on a nationalist identity and an anti-imperialist outlook. . |

| | |
|---|---|
| Protest | Protest expresses relatively overt reaction to events or situations: sometimes in favor, though more often opposed. protesters may organize a protest as a way of publicly and forcefully making their opinions heard in an attempt to influence public opinion or government policy, or may undertake direct action to attempt to directly enact desired changes themselves. |
| | Self-expression can, in theory, in practice or in appearance, be restricted by governmental policy, economic circumstances, religious orthodoxy, social structures, or media monopoly. |
| Revolution | A Revolution is a fundamental change in power or organizational structures that takes place in a relatively short period of time. Aristotle described two types of political Revolution |
| | · Complete change from one constitution to another<br>· Modification of an existing constitution.<br>Revolution s have occurred through human history and vary widely in terms of methods, duration, and motivating ideology. |
| Republic | A Republic is a form of government in which the head of state is not a monarch and the people (or at least a part of its people) have an impact on its government. The word "Republic" is derived from the Latin phrase res publica which can be translated as "public affairs".<br>Both modern and ancient Republics vary widely in their ideology and composition. |
| Austria-Hungary | Austria-Hungary the Dual Monarchy or the k.u.k Monarchy, was a state in Central Europe ruled by the House of Habsburg, constitutionally a monarchic union between the crowns of the Austrian Empire and the Kingdom of Hungary. The state was a result of the Ausgleich or Compromise of 1867, under which the Austrian Habsburgs agreed to share power with a separate Hungarian government, dividing the territory of the former Austrian Empire between them. The Dual Monarchy existed for 51 years until 1918, when it dissolved following military defeat in the First World War. |
| France | France or ; French: [fÈ É'Ìƒs]), officially the French Republic , is a country located in Western Europe, with several overseas islands and territories located on other continents. Metropolitan France extends from the Mediterranean Sea to the English Channel and the North Sea, and from the Rhine to the Atlantic Ocean. It is often referred to as L"Hexagone ("The Hexagon") because of the geometric shape of its territory. |
| Union of Soviet Socialist Republics | The Union of Soviet Socialist Republics (USSR) was a constitutionally socialist state that existed in Eurasia from 1922 to 1991. The name is a translation of the Russian: Â·), tr. Soyuz Sovetskikh Sotsialisticheskikh Respublik, abbreviated Ð¡Ð¡Ð¡Ð , SSSR. The common short name is Soviet Union, from Ð¡Ð¾Ð²ÐµÑ‚Ñ ÐºÐ¸Ð¹ Ð¡Ð¾ÑŽÐ··, Sovetskiy Soyuz. |
| Communist Party | A political party described as a Communist Party includes those that advocate the application of the social principles of communism through a communist form of government. The name originates from the 1848 tract Manifesto of the Communist Party by Karl Marx, Friedrich Engels. The Leninist concept of a Communist Party encompases a larger political system and includes not only an ideological orientation but also a wide set of organizational policies. |

| | |
|---|---|
| Nation | A nation is a body of people who share a real or imagined common history, culture, language or ethnic origin, who typically inhabit a particular country or territory. The development and conceptualization of the nation is closely related to the development of modern industrial states and nationalist movements in Europe in the 18th and 19th centuries, although nationalists would trace nations into the past along an uninterrupted lines of historical narrative. |
| | Benedict Anderson argued that nations were "imagined communities" because "the members of even the smallest nation will never know most of their fellow-members, meet them, or even hear of them, yet in the minds of each lives the image of their communion", and traced their origins back to vernacular print journalism, which by its very nature was limited with linguistic zones and addressed a common audience. |
| German Democratic Republic | The German Democratic Republic was a self-declared socialist state (but commonly referred to in the West as a communist state) that originated from the Soviet Zone of occupied Germany and the Soviet sector of occupied Berlin. The German Democratic Republic existed from 7 October 1949 until 3 October 1990, when its re-established states acceded to the adjacent Federal Republic of Germany, thus producing the current form of Germany. During its existence, the German Democratic Republic was a member of the Eastern Bloc of eastern European nations that were aligned with the Soviet Union . |
| Prague Spring | The Prague Spring (Czech: PraÅ¾ské jaro, Slovak: PraÅ¾ská jar) was a period of political liberalization in Czechoslovakia during the era of its domination by the Soviet Union after World War II. It began on 5 January 1968, when reformist Slovak Alexander DubÄ ek came to power, and continued until 21 August when the Soviet Union and members of its Warsaw Pact allies invaded the country to halt the reforms. |
| | The Prague Spring reforms were an attempt by DubÄ ek to grant additional rights to the citizens in an act of partial decentralization of the economy and democratization. The freedoms granted included a loosening of restrictions on the media, speech and travel. |
| Solidarity | Solidarity is a Polish trade union federation founded in September 1980 at the GdaÅ„sk Shipyard, and originally led by Lech WaÅ‚Ä™sa. |
| | Solidarity was the first non-Communist-controlled trade union in a Warsaw Pact country. In the 1980s it constituted a broad anti-bureaucratic social movement. |
| Irish Republican Army | The Irish Republican Army (Irish: Óglaigh na hÉireann) was an Irish republican revolutionary military organisation descended from the Irish Volunteers, established 25 November 1913 and who in April 1916 staged the Easter Rising. The Irish Volunteers were recognised in 1919 by Dáil Éireann (its elected assembly) as the legitimate army of the unilaterally declared Irish Republic, the Irish state proclaimed at Easter in 1916 and reaffirmed by the Dáil in January 1919. Thereafter, the Irish Republican Army waged a guerrilla campaign against British rule in Ireland in the Irish War of Independence from 1919-1921. |

| | |
|---|---|
| Rebellion | Rebellion is a refusal of obedience. It may, therefore, be seen as encompassing a range of behaviors from civil disobedience and mass nonviolent resistance, to violent and organized attempts to destroy an established authority such as the government. Those who participate in Rebellions are known as "rebels". |
| Roman | A Roman or civil diocese was one of the administrative divisions of the later Roman Empire, starting with the Tetrarchy. It formed the intermediate level of government, grouping several provinces and being in turn subordinated to a praetorian prefecture. The earliest use of "diocese" as an administrative unit was in the Greek-speaking East. |
| Social Democratic Party | The Social Democratic Party (Romanian: Partidul Social Democrat, PSD) is a major political party of Romania. It can be loosely classified as a center-left party, although the right-left division in Romania is quite blurred. After the 2008 Romanian legislative elections the party entered in coalition with the Democratic Liberal Party (PD-L) and formed a government led by Emil Boc, the president of the PD-L. Previously, from 2005 to 2008, the PSD was an opposition party, after it lost the 2004 legislative election to the now-defunct Justice and Truth Alliance, comprising the National Liberal Party and Democratic Party. |
| Italy | Italy (Italian: Italia), officially the Italian Republic (Italian: Repubblica Italiana), is a country located on the Italian Peninsula in Southern Europe and on the two largest islands in the Mediterranean Sea, Sicily and Sardinia. Italy shares its northern, Alpine boundary with France, Switzerland, Austria and Slovenia. The independent states of San Marino and the Vatican City are enclaves within the Italian Peninsula, and Campione d"Italia is an Italian exclave in Switzerland. |
| Canada | CANADA is a country occupying most of northern North America, extending from the Atlantic Ocean in the east to the Pacific Ocean in the west and northward into the Arctic Ocean. It is the world"s second largest country by total area and shares the world"s longest common border with the United States to the south and northwest. The land occupied by CANADA was inhabited for millennia by various groups of Aboriginal people. |
| J. Robert Oppenheimer | J. Robert Oppenheimer (April 22, 1904 - February 18, 1967) was an American theoretical physicist and professor of physics at the University of California, Berkeley. He is best known for his role as the scientific director of the Manhattan Project, the World War II effort to develop the first nuclear weapons at the secret Los Alamos National Laboratory in New Mexico. For this reason he is remembered as "The Father of the Atomic Bomb". |
| Green Party | A Green Party or ecologist party is a formally organized political party based on the principles of Green politics. These principles include environmentalism, reliance on grassroots democracy, nonviolence, and support for social justice causes, including those related to the rights of indigenous peoples, among others. "Greens" believe that the exercise of these principles leads to the health of people, societies, and ecosystems. |

History

· History of the East Coast of the United States
· History of the Southern United States
· History of the United States
· List of National Historic Landmarks in North Carolina
· National Register of Historic Places listings in North Carolina

Regions

Larger cities

Smaller cities

Major Towns

Counties

Michael

Michael is a given name that comes from the Hebrew: žÖ´×™×›Ö¸× Öµ×œ / ×ž×™×›×›× ×œ×â€Ž , meaning "Who is like God?" In English, it is sometimes shortened to Mike, Mikey, or, especially in Ireland, Mick.

Michael is one of the Archangels.

Female forms of Michael include Michele, Michelle, Michaela, Mechelle, Micheline, and Michaelle, although there are women with the name Michael, such as Michael Learned.

Peasant

A Peasant is an agricultural worker who subsists by working a small plot of ground. The term Peasant today is sometimes used in a pejorative sense for impoverished farmers.

Peasants typically make up the majority of the agricultural labour force in a Pre-industrial society, dependent on the cultivation of their land: without stockpiles of provisions they thrive or starve according to the most recent harvest.

Communist Party

A political party described as a Communist Party includes those that advocate the application of the social principles of communism through a communist form of government. The name originates from the 1848 tract Manifesto of the Communist Party by Karl Marx, Friedrich Engels. The Leninist concept of a Communist Party encompasses a larger political system and includes not only an ideological orientation but also a wide set of organizational policies.

Congress

The 2001 Congress of the Greens/Green Party USA, held at Carbondale, Illinois, was a critical event in the history of the Green Party in the United States. At the Congress, occurring July 20 to July 23, at which the G/GPUSA was to consider the Boston Proposal , a tentative "merger" agreement between it and the Association of State Green Parties (ASGP). After an intense internal organizational struggle, most of which revolved around whether or not to "accredit" various delegations (and thus grant the individuals within them voting privileges), the proposal was rejected; although 55% of the members in attendance voted to approve it (99 in favor, 81 against), the organization"s bylaws required yes votes from a "super-majority" of 66.7% of the delegates in attendance to pass.

France

France or ; French: [fÊ É¹fs]), officially the French Republic , is a country located in Western Europe, with several overseas islands and territories located on other continents. Metropolitan France extends from the Mediterranean Sea to the English Channel and the North Sea, and from the Rhine to the Atlantic Ocean. It is often referred to as L"Hexagone ("The Hexagon") because of the geometric shape of its territory.

Revolution

A Revolution is a fundamental change in power or organizational structures that takes place in a relatively short period of time. Aristotle described two types of political Revolution

· Complete change from one constitution to another
· Modification of an existing constitution.
Revolution s have occurred through human history and vary widely in terms of methods, duration, and motivating ideology.

Czechoslovakia

Czechoslovakia was a sovereign state in Central Europe which existed from October 1918, when it declared its independence from the Austro-Hungarian Empire, until 1992. From 1939 to 1945 the state did not have a de facto existence, due to its forced division and partial incorporation into Germany, but the Czech government-in-exile nevertheless continued to exist during this time period while Slovakia was independent from the Czech part. On 1 January 1993 Czechoslovakia peacefully split into the Czech Republic and Slovakia.

Republic

A Republic is a form of government in which the head of state is not a monarch and the people (or at least a part of its people) have an impact on its government. The word "Republic" is derived from the Latin phrase res publica which can be translated as "public affairs".
Both modern and ancient Republics vary widely in their ideology and composition.

Roman

A Roman or civil diocese was one of the administrative divisions of the later Roman Empire, starting with the Tetrarchy. It formed the intermediate level of government, grouping several provinces and being in turn subordinated to a praetorian prefecture.
The earliest use of "diocese" as an administrative unit was in the Greek-speaking East.

| | |
|---|---|
| Solidarity | Solidarity is a Polish trade union federation founded in September 1980 at the GdaÅ„sk Shipyard, and originally led by Lech WaÅ‚Ä™sa.<br><br>Solidarity was the first non-Communist-controlled trade union in a Warsaw Pact country. In the 1980s it constituted a broad anti-bureaucratic social movement. |
| German Democratic Republic | The German Democratic Republic was a self-declared socialist state (but commonly referred to in the West as a communist state) that originated from the Soviet Zone of occupied Germany and the Soviet sector of occupied Berlin. The German Democratic Republic existed from 7 October 1949 until 3 October 1990, when its re-established states acceded to the adjacent Federal Republic of Germany, thus producing the current form of Germany. During its existence, the German Democratic Republic was a member of the Eastern Bloc of eastern European nations that were aligned with the Soviet Union. |
| Koinon | The Koinon (or "League") of Free Laconians was established in 21 BC by the Emperor Augustus, giving formal structure to a group of cities that had been associated for almost two centuries.<br><br>The Eleutherolakones (á¼˜λευθερολÎ¬κωνες, free Laconians) are first mentioned in 195 BC, after Sparta"s defeat in the Roman-Spartan War. The Roman general Titus Quinctius Flaminius placed several coastal cities of the Mani Peninsula under the protection of the Achean League, freeing them from Spartan hegemony. |
| Yugoslavia | Yugoslavia is a term that describes three political entities that existed successively on the Balkan Peninsula in Europe, during most of the 20th century.<br><br>The first country to be known by this name was the Kingdom of Yugoslavia which before 3 October 1929 was known as the Kingdom of Serbs, Croats and Slovenes. It was established on 1 December 1918 by the union of the State of Slovenes, Croats and Serbs and the Kingdom of Serbia. |
| Bosnian War | The Bosnian War was an international armed conflict that took place between March 1992 and November 1995. The war involved several sides. According to numerous International Criminal Tribunal for the former Yugoslavia judgements the conflict involved Bosnia and the Federal Republic of Yugoslavia as well as Croatia. |
| Montenegro | Montenegro ( or /ËŒmÉ›'ntÉ"Ë‡niÉ" É¡roËŠ/), ) (meaning "Black Mountain" in Montenegrin) is a country located in Southeastern Europe. It has a coast on the Adriatic Sea to the south-west and is bordered by Croatia to the west, Bosnia and Herzegovina to the northwest, Serbia to the northeast, Kosovo to the east and Albania to the south . Its capital and largest city is Podgorica, while Cetinje is designated as the Prijestonica (ÐŸÑ€Ð¸Ñ˜ÐµÑ Ñ‚Ð¾Ð½Ð¸Ñ†Ð°), meaning the former Royal Capital City.. |
| Social Democratic Party | The Social Democratic Party (Romanian: Partidul Social Democrat, PSD) is a major political party of Romania. It can be loosely classified as a center-left party, although the right-left division in Romania is quite blurred. After the 2008 Romanian legislative elections the party entered in coalition with the Democratic Liberal Party (PD-L) and formed a government led by Emil Boc, the president of the PD-L. |

| | |
|---|---|
| | Previously, from 2005 to 2008, the PSD was an opposition party, after it lost the 2004 legislative election to the now-defunct Justice and Truth Alliance, comprising the National Liberal Party and Democratic Party. |
| Maastricht Treaty | The Maastricht Treaty (formally, the Treaty on European Union, TEU) was signed on 7 February 1992 in Maastricht, the Netherlands after final negotiations on 9 December 1991 between the members of the European Community and entered into force on 1 November 1993 during the Delors Commission. It created the European Union and led to the creation of the euro. The Maastricht Treaty has been amended to a degree by later treaties. |
| Cyprus | Cyprus , officially the Republic of Cyprus , is a Eurasian island country situated in the eastern Mediterranean, south of Turkey and west of Syria and Lebanon. Cyprus is the Mediterranean"s third largest island, and one of its most popular tourist destinations, attracting over 2.4 million tourists per year. A former British colony, it became an independent republic in 1960 and a member of the Commonwealth in 1961. |
| Canada | CANADA is a country occupying most of northern North America, extending from the Atlantic Ocean in the east to the Pacific Ocean in the west and northward into the Arctic Ocean. It is the world"s second largest country by total area and shares the world"s longest common border with the United States to the south and northwest. The land occupied by CANADA was inhabited for millennia by various groups of Aboriginal people. |
| Force | In physics, a Force is any external agent that causes a change in the motion of a free body, or that causes stress in a fixed body. It can also be described by intuitive concepts such as a push or pull that can cause an object with mass to change its velocity , i.e., to accelerate, or which can cause a flexible object to deform. Force has both magnitude and direction, making it a vector quantity. |
| Irish Republican Army | The Irish Republican Army (Irish: Óglaigh na hÉireann) was an Irish republican revolutionary military organisation descended from the Irish Volunteers, established 25 November 1913 and who in April 1916 staged the Easter Rising. The Irish Volunteers were recognised in 1919 by Dáil Éireann (its elected assembly) as the legitimate army of the unilaterally declared Irish Republic, the Irish state proclaimed at Easter in 1916 and reaffirmed by the Dáil in January 1919. Thereafter, the Irish Republican Army waged a guerrilla campaign against British rule in Ireland in the Irish War of Independence from 1919-1921. |
| New Order | New Order were an English musical group formed in 1980 by Bernard Sumner , Peter Hook (bass, backing vocals, electronic drums) and Stephen Morris (drums, synthesizers.) New Order were formed in the wake of the demise of their previous group Joy Division, following the suicide of vocalist Ian Curtis. They were soon joined by additional keyboardist Gillian Gilbert. |
| North Atlantic Treaty | The North Atlantic Treaty is the treaty that brought North Atlantic Treaty O into existence, signed in Washington, DC on April 4, 1949. The original twelve nations that signed it and thus became the founding members of North Atlantic Treaty O were: Map of North Atlantic Treaty O countries chronological membership. |

Later the following nations joined:
When Germany was reunified in 1990, the country as a whole became a member of North Atlantic Treaty O.
During the April 2008 summit in Bucharest, Croatia and Albania were officially invited to join North Atlantic Treaty O. They both signed the treaty and officially joined North Atlantic Treaty O on April 1st, 2009

**September**

September Â·) is the ninth month of the year in the Gregorian Calendar and one of four Gregorian months with 30 days.
In Latin, septem means "seven" and septimus means "seventh"; September was in fact the seventh month of the Roman calendar until 153 BC, when the first month changed from Kalendas Martius to Kalendas Januarius (1 January). In the Northern hemisphere, the beginning of the meteorological autumn is 1 September.

**Protest**

Protest expresses relatively overt reaction to events or situations: sometimes in favor, though more often opposed. protesters may organize a protest as a way of publicly and forcefully making their opinions heard in an attempt to influence public opinion or government policy, or may undertake direct action to attempt to directly enact desired changes themselves.
Self-expression can, in theory, in practice or in appearance, be restricted by governmental policy, economic circumstances, religious orthodoxy, social structures, or media monopoly.

**Liberation movement**

A Liberation movement is an organization fighting a rebellion against a colonial power, often seeking independence based on a nationalist identity and an anti-imperialist outlook. .

**Green Party**

A Green Party or ecologist party is a formally organized political party based on the principles of Green politics. These principles include environmentalism, reliance on grassroots democracy, nonviolence, and support for social justice causes, including those related to the rights of indigenous peoples, among others. "Greens" believe that the exercise of these principles leads to the health of people, societies, and ecosystems.

**Nation**

A nation is a body of people who share a real or imagined common history, culture, language or ethnic origin, who typically inhabit a particular country or territory. The development and conceptualization of the nation is closely related to the development of modern industrial states and nationalist movements in Europe in the 18th and 19th centuries, although nationalists would trace nations into the past along an uninterrupted lines of historical narrative.
Benedict Anderson argued that nations were "imagined communities" because "the members of even the smallest nation will never know most of their fellow-members, meet them, or even hear of them, yet in the minds of each lives the image of their communion", and traced their origins back to vernacular print journalism, which by its very nature was limited with linguistic zones and addressed a common audience.

Law

The great end, for which men entered into society, was to secure their property. That right is preserved sacred and incommunicable in all instances, where it has not been taken away or abridged by some public Law for the good of the whole ... If no excuse can be found or produced, the silence of the books is an authority against the defendant, and the plaintiff must have judgment.

Internet

The Internet is a global system of interconnected computer networks that use the standardized Internet Protocol Suite (TCP/IP), serving billions of users worldwide. It is a network of networks that consists of millions of private and public, academic, business, and government networks of local to global scope that are linked by copper wires, fiber-optic cables, wireless connections, and other technologies. The Internet carries a vast array of information resources and services, most notably the inter-linked hypertext documents of the World Wide Web (WWW) and the infrastructure to support electronic mail.

CPSIA information can be obtained at www.ICGtesting.com
Printed in the USA
239967LV00002B/80/P